Copyright© 2019 by Breece A. Perry

Photography & Illustration Copyright©2019 by Breece A. Perry

All rights reserved.

Other than excerpts for purpose of review, no works within this publication are to be used separately without explicit permission, reproduced or sold in part or whole for profit.

HoneyBee Books:

<u>Artist, Photographer, Book Design</u>
Breece A. Perry

<u>Editor</u>
Breece A. Perry

<u>Producer</u>
Melissa L. Perez

First Edition October 2019

Introduction

     These old sketch books are beginning to succumb to the decay of time. Second time going through the old sketch books and what a journey down memory lane. This is the follow up to the color book. This book will contain a few selected pencil sketches, incomplete color illustrations, and black and white.

     These are my favorite and most age appropriate. Thirty years of drawing in sketch books or on random sheets of blank paper. With a lot of help, Melissa kept me focused with the daunting task of putting it all together for a second time.

     While viewing this book, take notice of the transition from sketch to ink line to color. Many of the unfinished works show this transition. Having todays hand held communication devices made it very easy to take photos (with out having to develop your own 35mm film or have a photo place ruin the only evidence of the film roll). Being a photographer prior to digital was very expensive and hazardous. The standards of today click a photo and trash it in a few seconds, seems to take too long. Anyone who has taken the time to set an aperture and spend any time in a darkroom understands this. So with this said, I really enjoyed taking photos throughout the progression from rough sketch to ink then finally color. In doing so realized that most of the early drawings must be preserved digitally, so in my later years I will be able to turn page by page and recall a simpler time.

     All drawings are done with pencil, ink, color markers and color pencils.

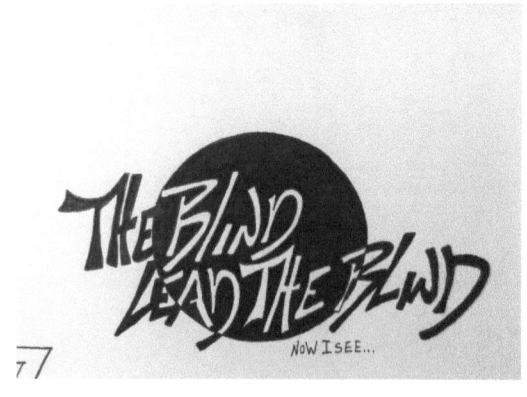

5 inches x 3 inches   1994

Looking back at the beginning and moving forward again. First page in the earliest sketch book, pencil and color pencils.

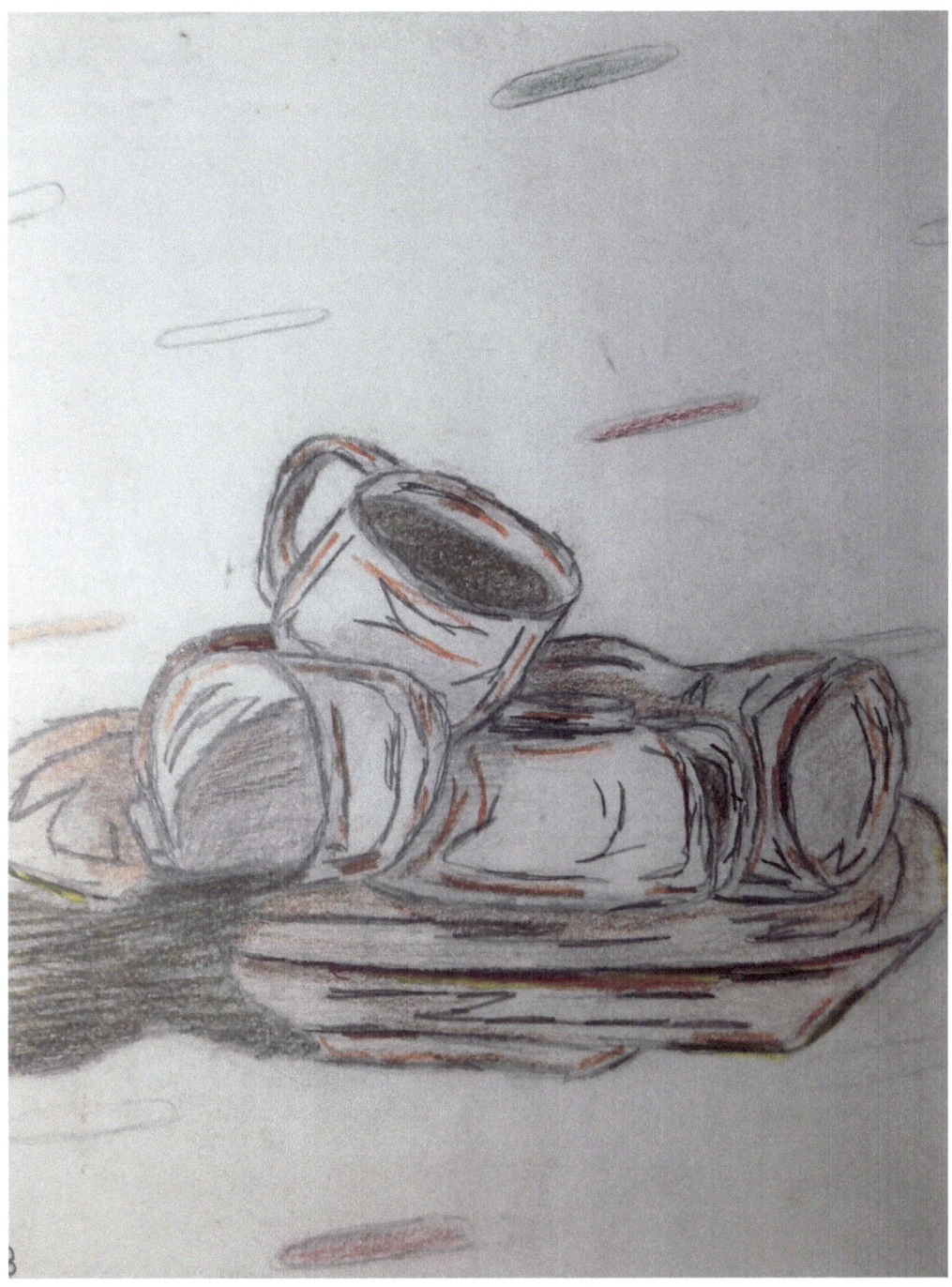

Tea Cups and Bottle on Plate   1989   8 inches x 11 inches

I really enjoyed drawing in a surrealist style early in the development towards a unique drawing style, being so young and wanting to succeed as an artist. With this style of drawing there really is no correct way or wrong way. This is a favorite of mine a few landscapes that follow one another in the sketch book. Also a way to put some odd doodles together on a big sheet of blank space.

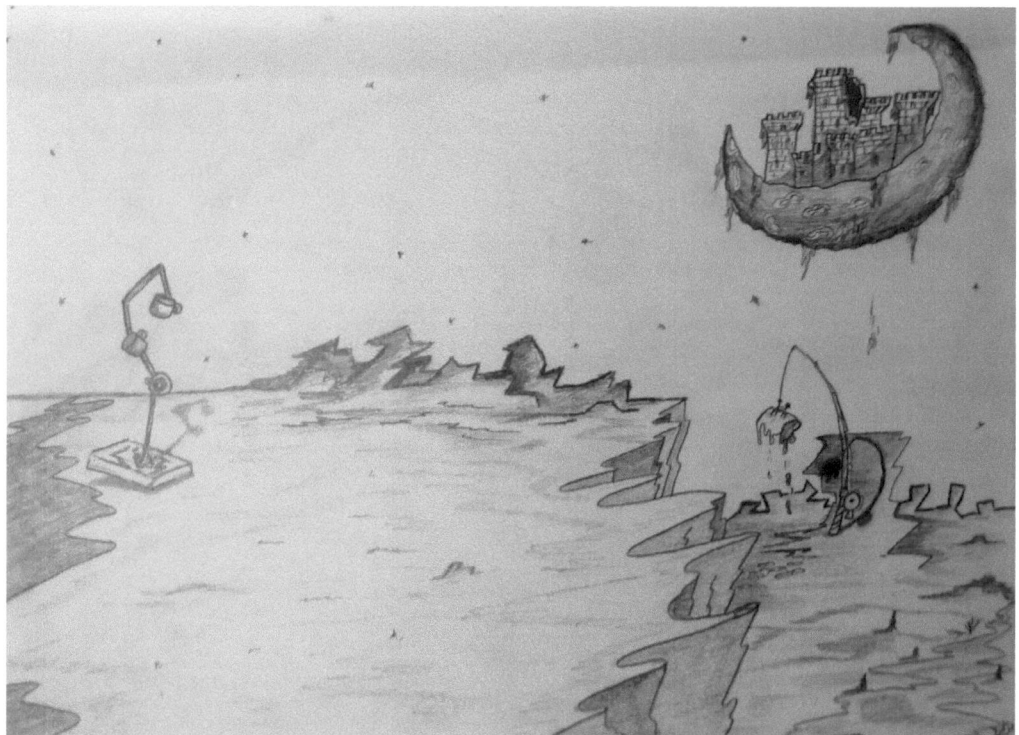

Fishing the Coffee Canyon   1989   8 inches x 11 inches

After a few pages of just weird landscapes you turn a page to find some doodles. i must have done these to make myself laugh. School was streamlining art styles saying what what art is and what is not art. Always a fascinating debate. Being defiant like many artist before me and many more to follow, I draw to make myself laugh for myself. Not being told what to draw or what art means to them.

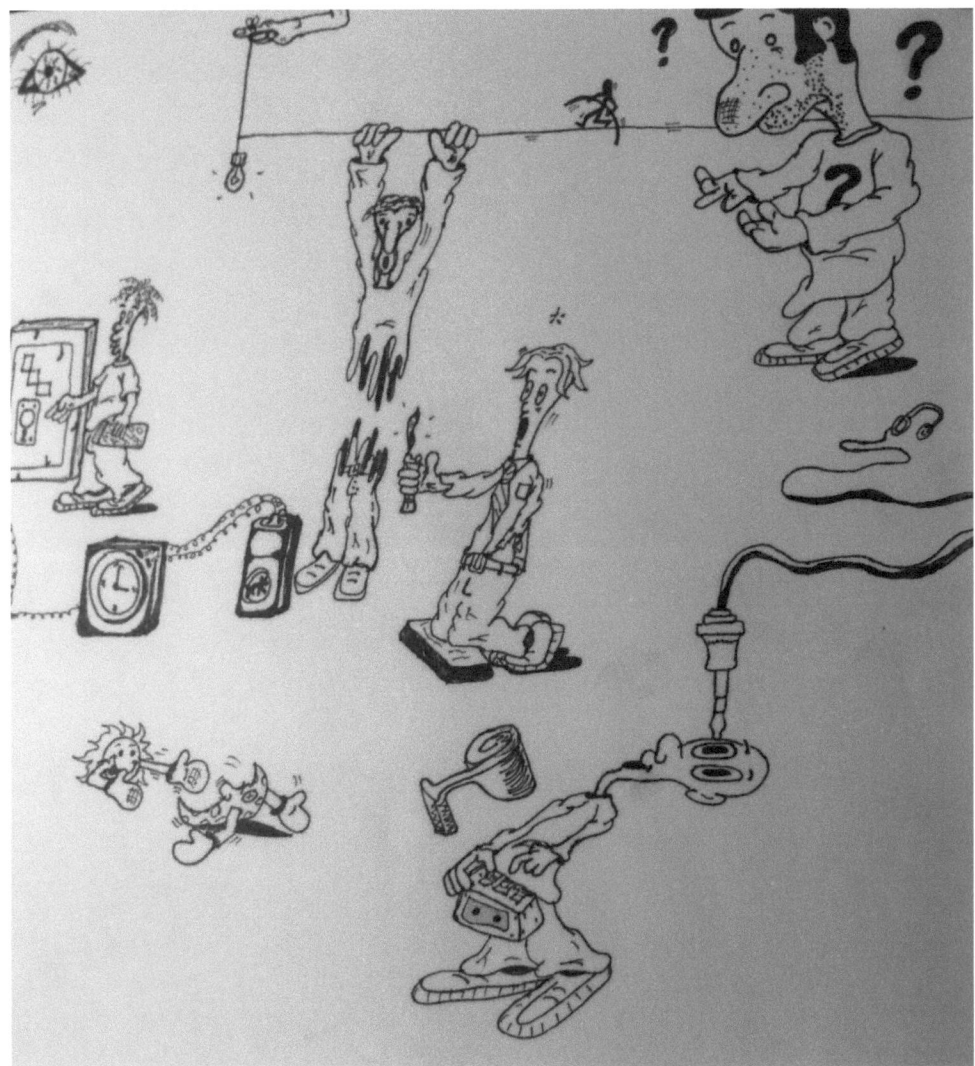

Moving on From Landscapes   1989   8 inches x 8 inches

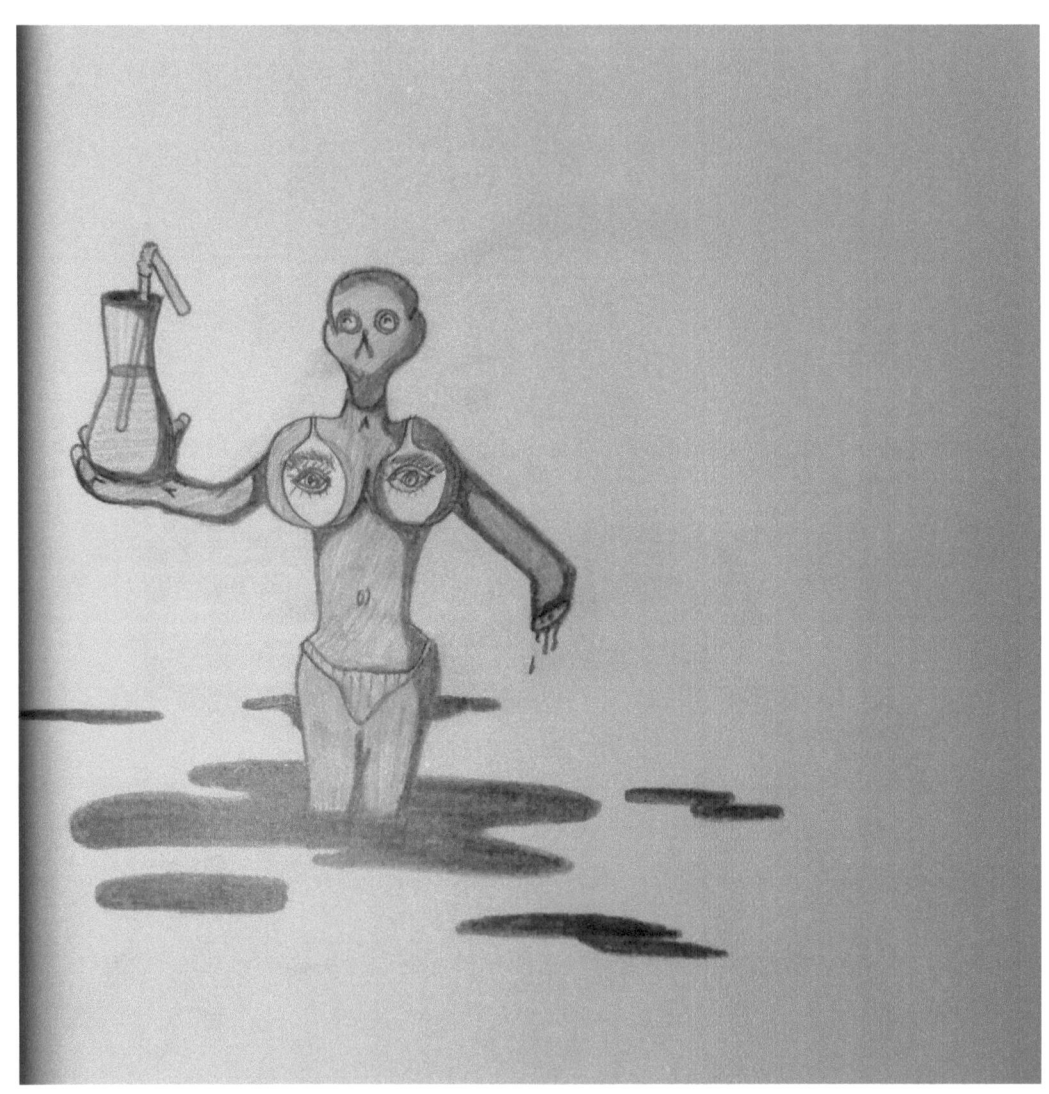

Lemonade in the Shallows 1989 6 inches x 5 inches

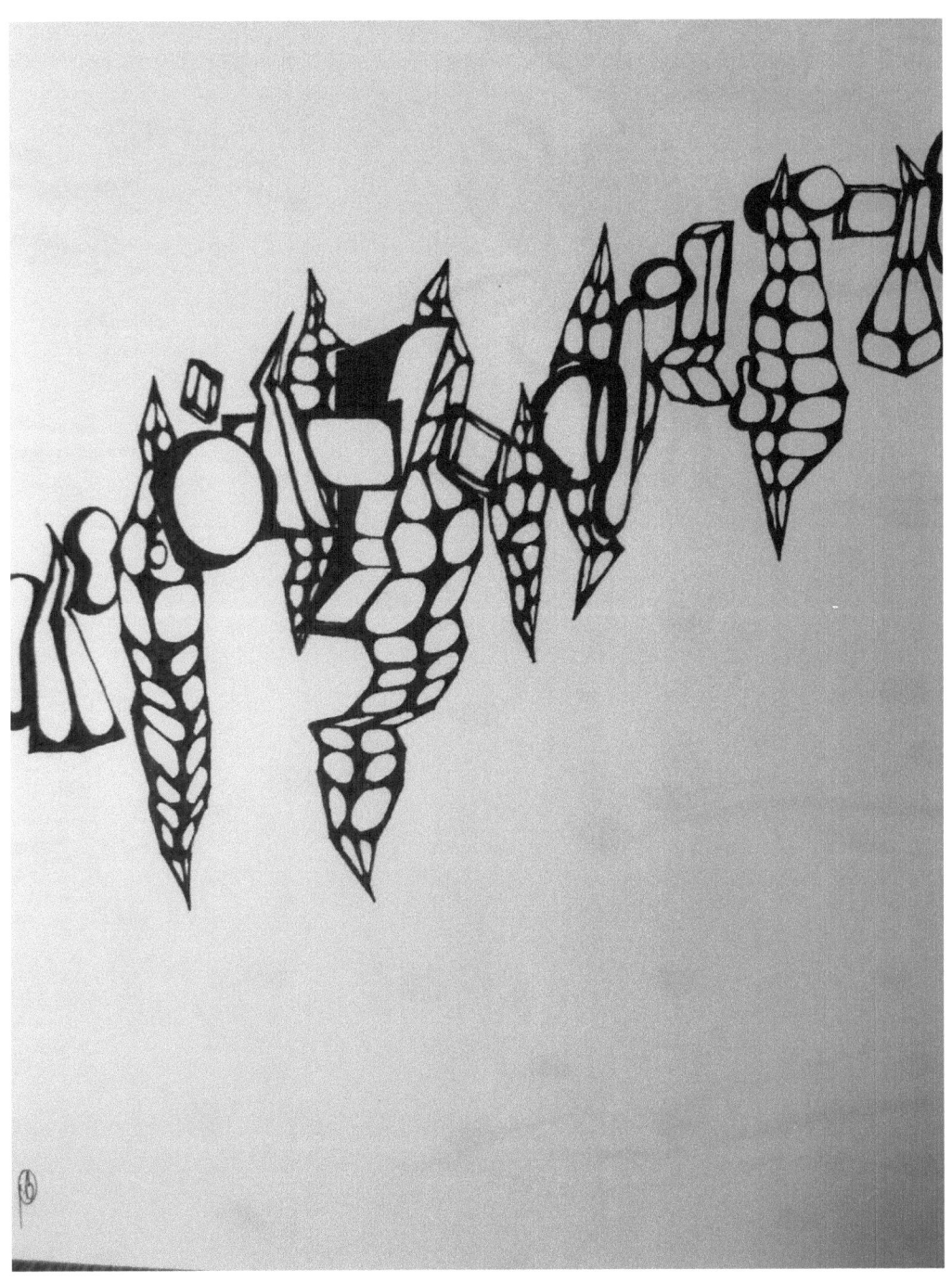

Constant Elevation 1989 8 inches x 8 inches

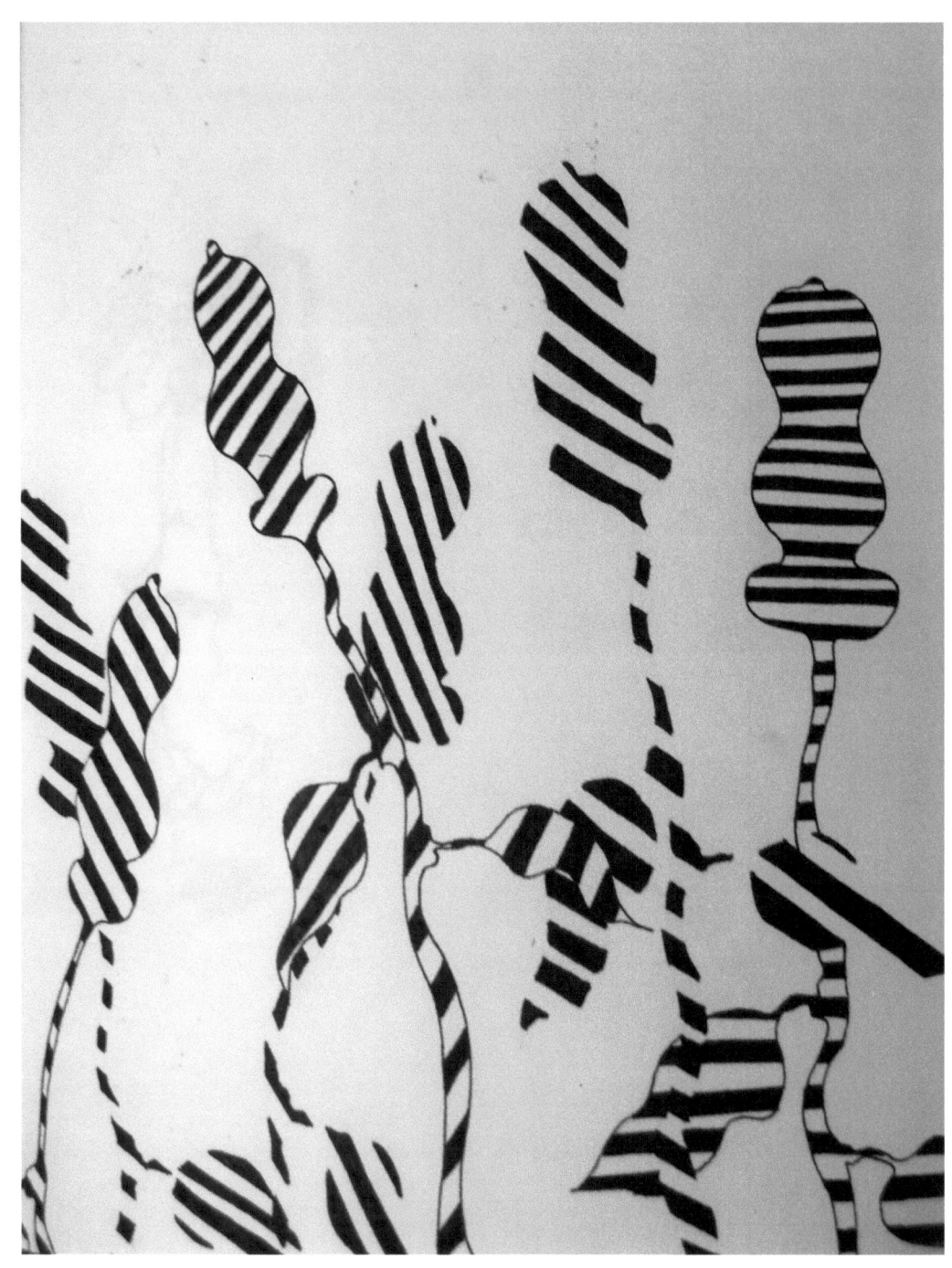

Sprouts — 1989 — 8 inches x 9 inches

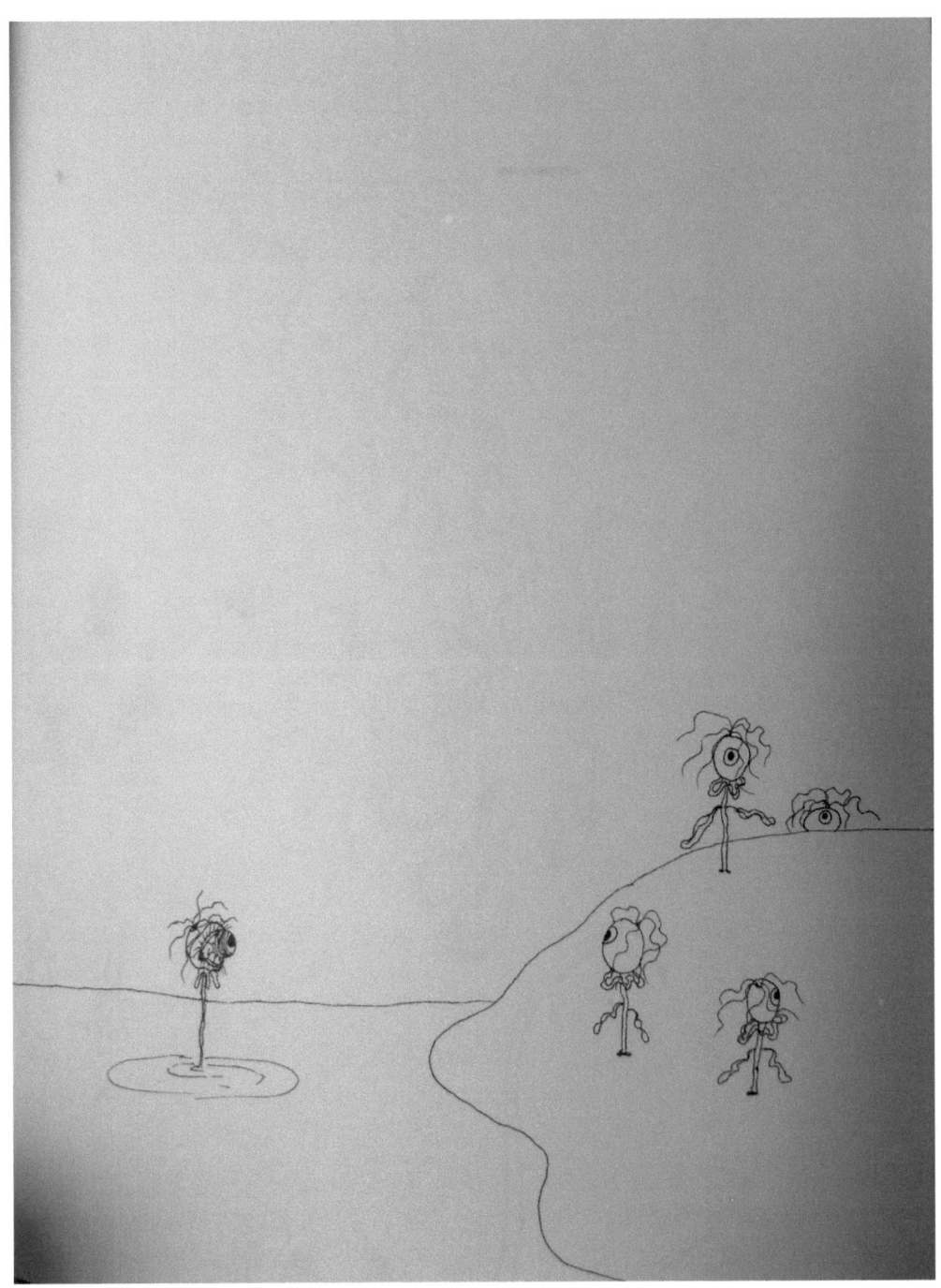

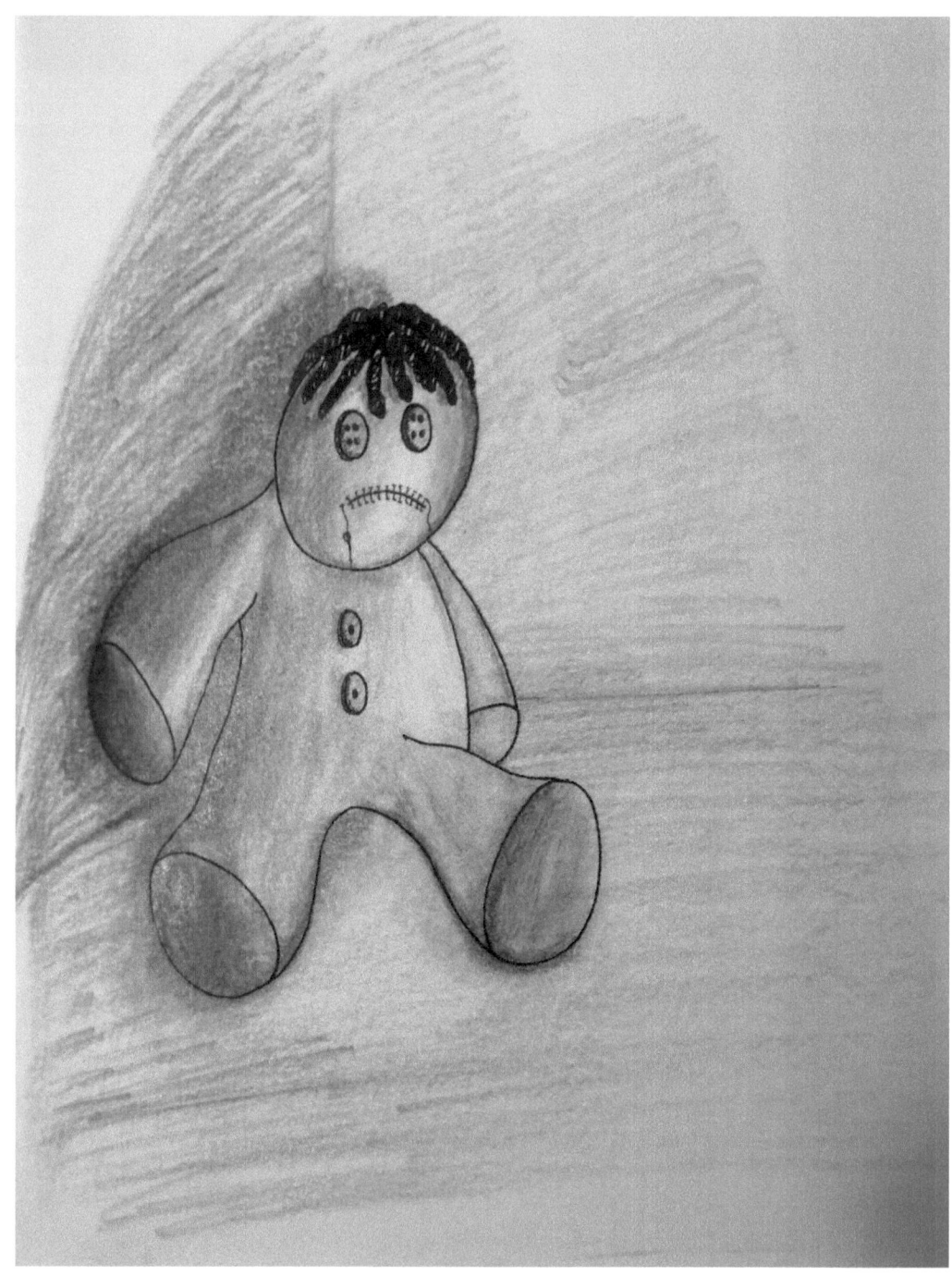

Seen and Not Heard   1989   7 inches x 9 inches

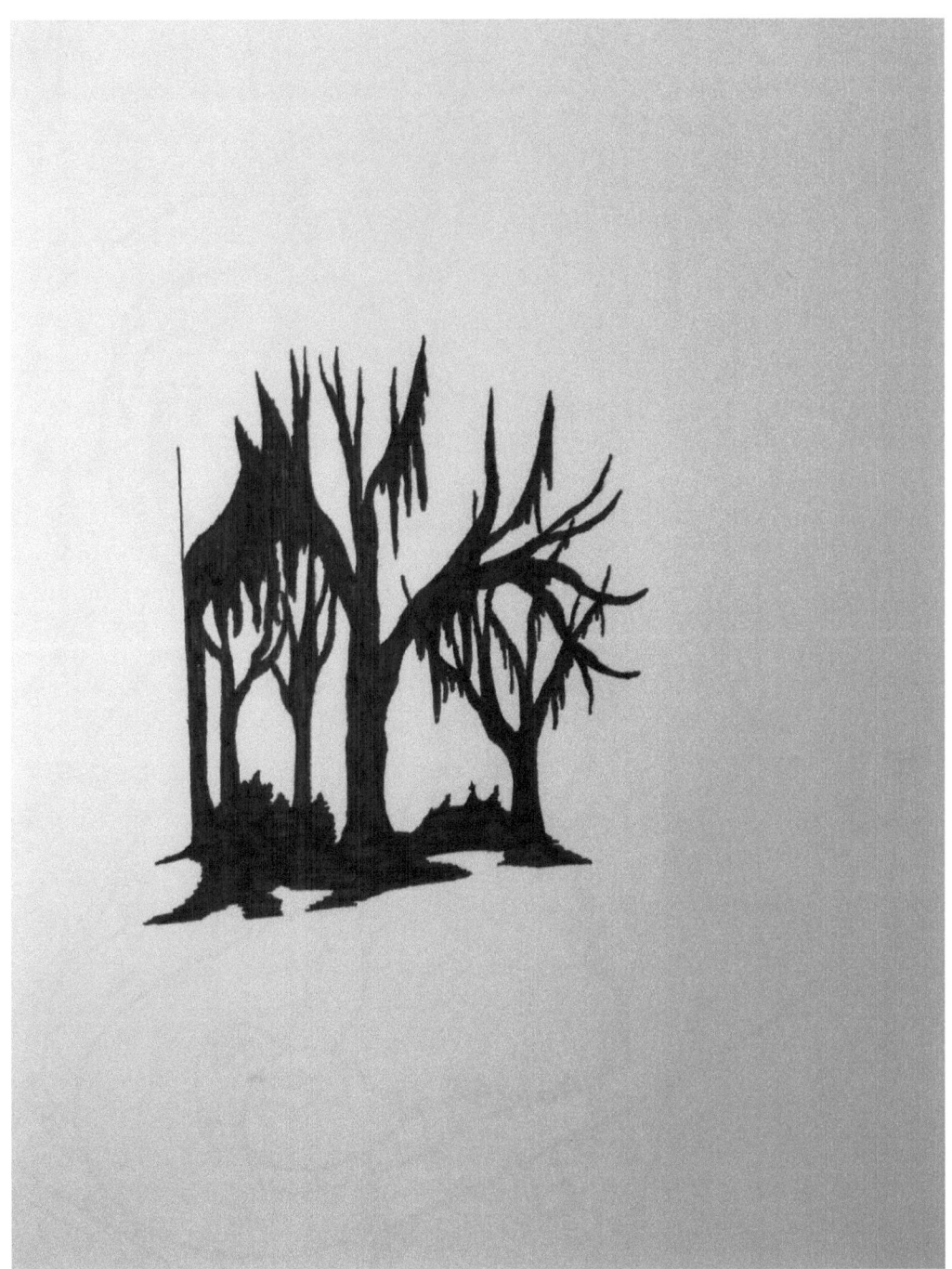

Southern Trees 1989 5 inches x 5 inches

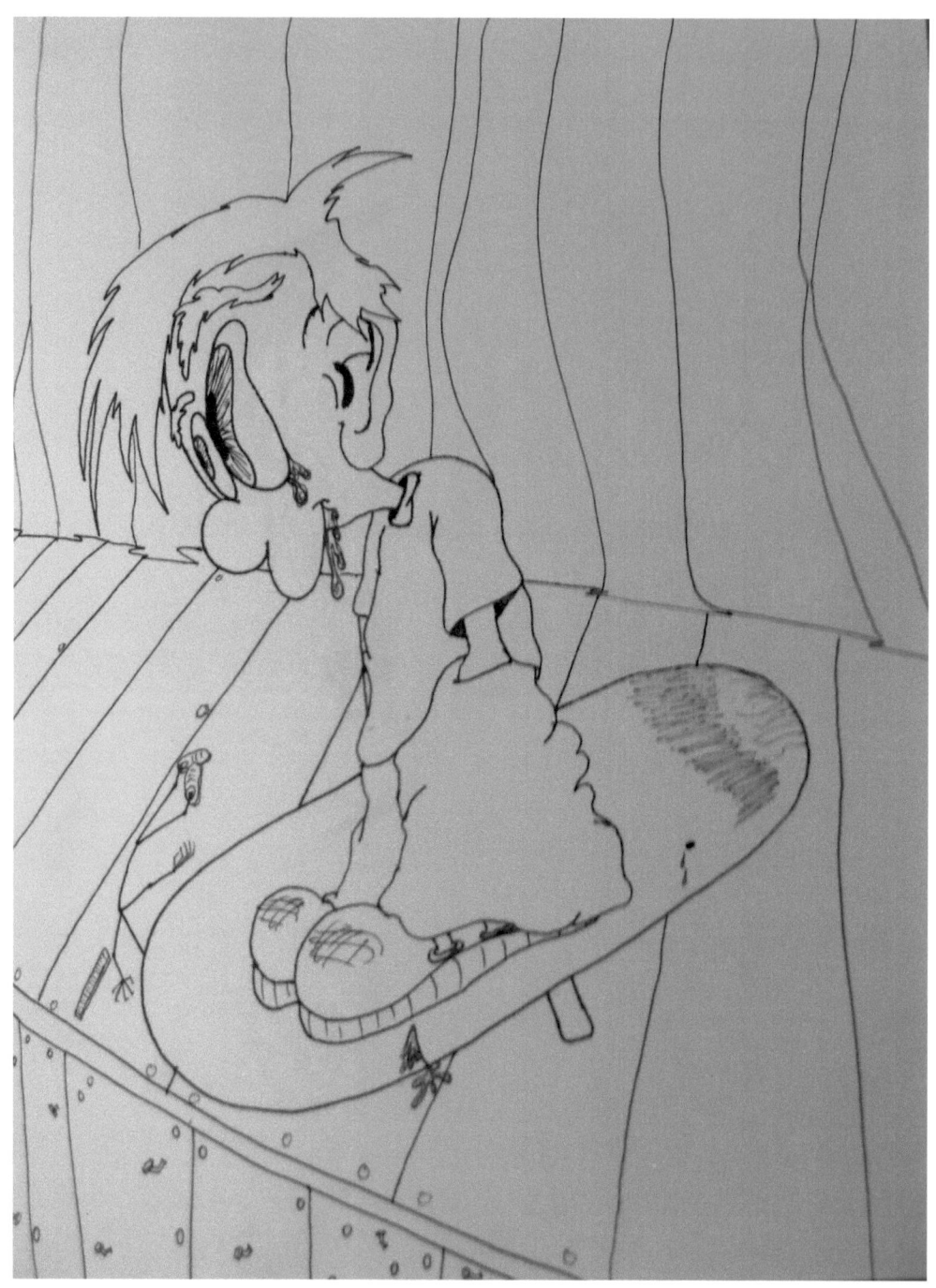

School Flat Out Boring   1989   8 inches x 11 inches

This is the first drawing in the second sketch book. Back to some basic landscapes. Testing out the boundaries of the smaller book.

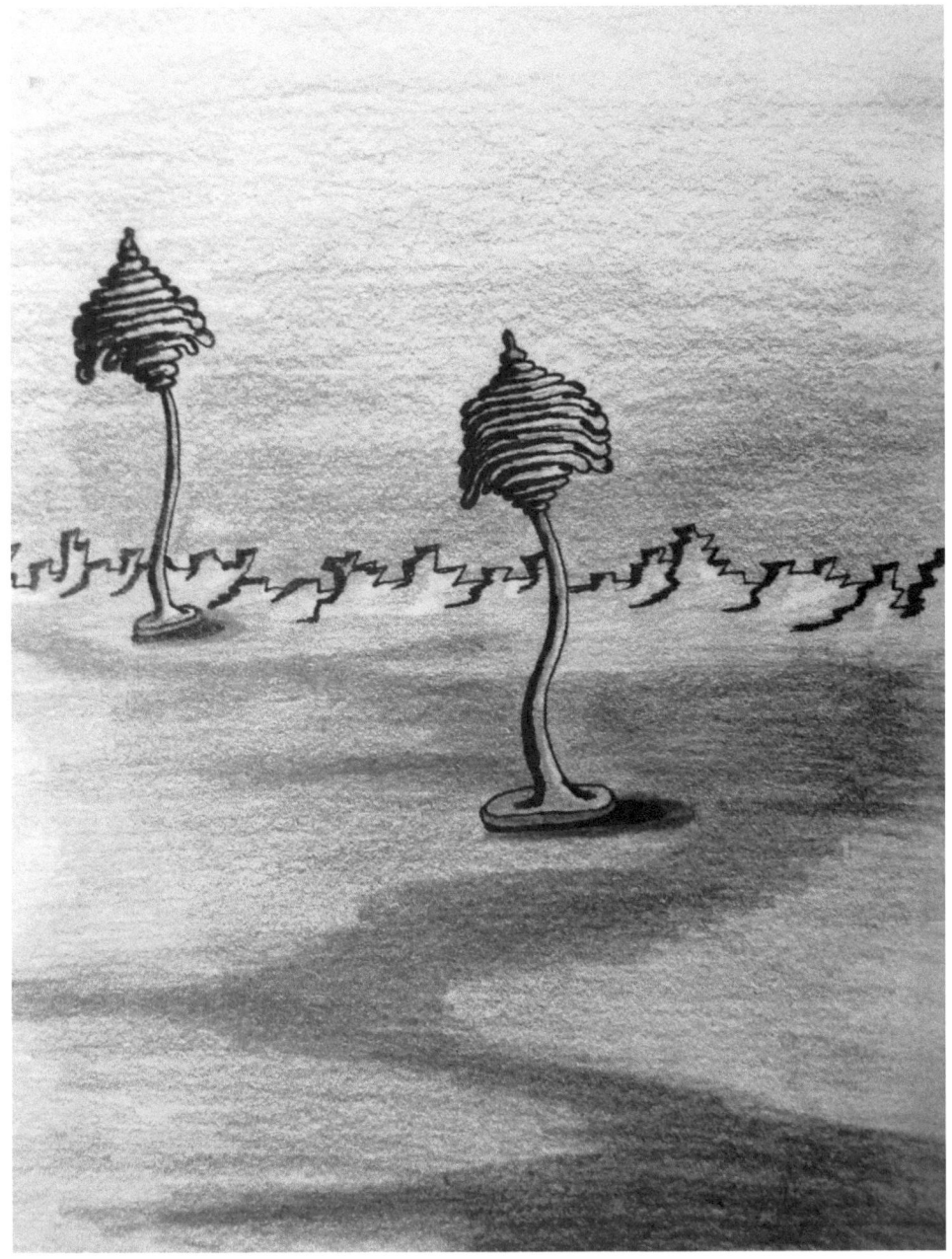

Broken Landscape   1989   6 inches x 9 inches

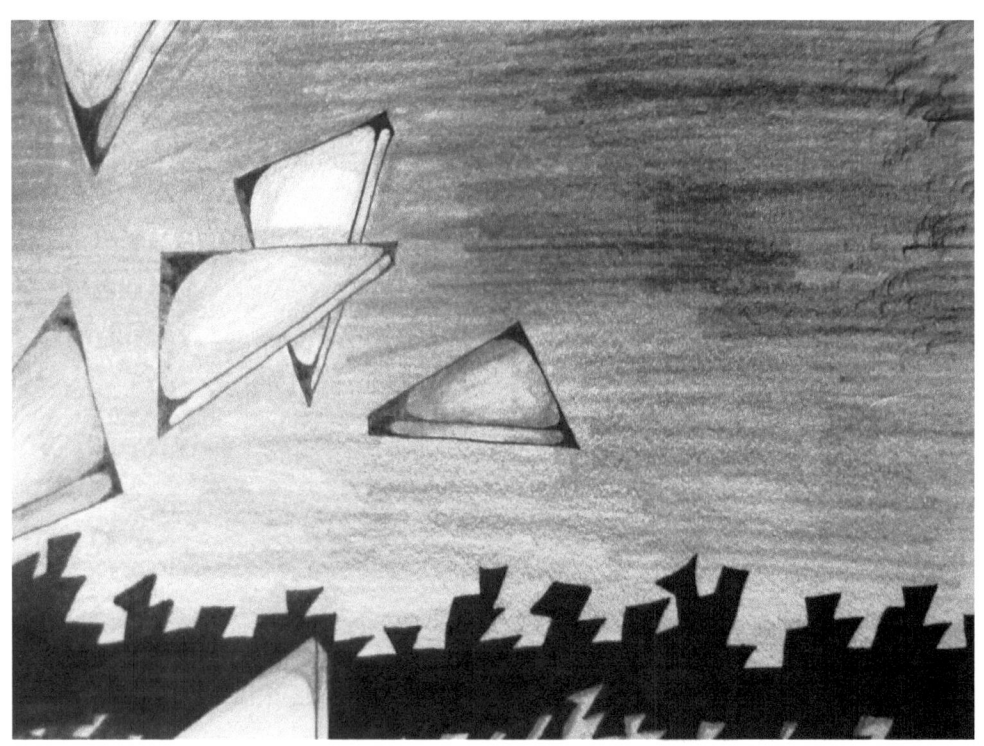

Pencil Ink Triangles   1989   6 inches x 9 inches

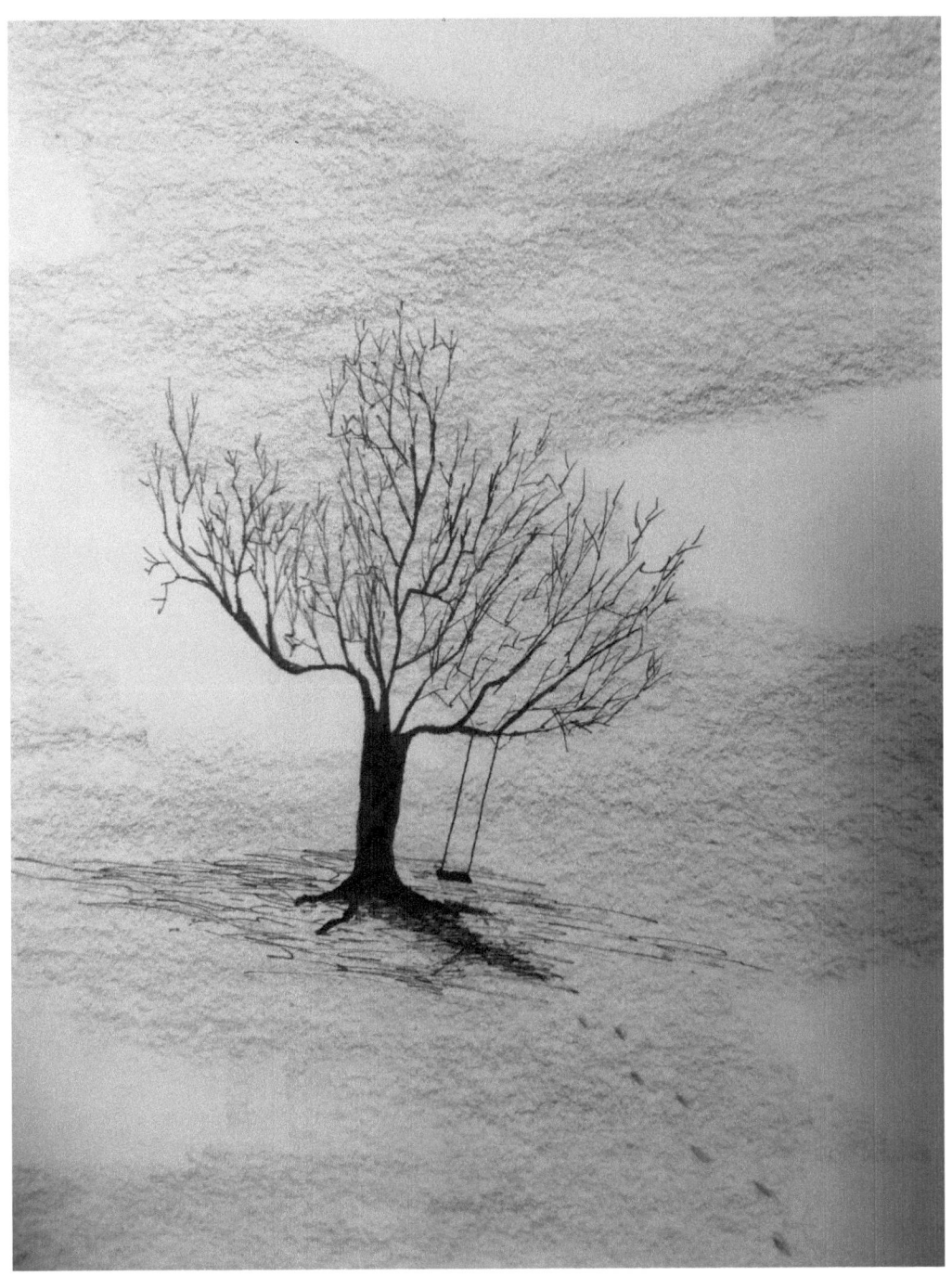

Seasonal Swing — 1989 — 6 inches x 9 inches

Anyone who is in this predicament or has been will understand this desire to have when you have not. Always dream big, because what your dreams manifest is always more than what you have had you not dared to dream at all. In negative surroundings you can be the change, so stay positive.

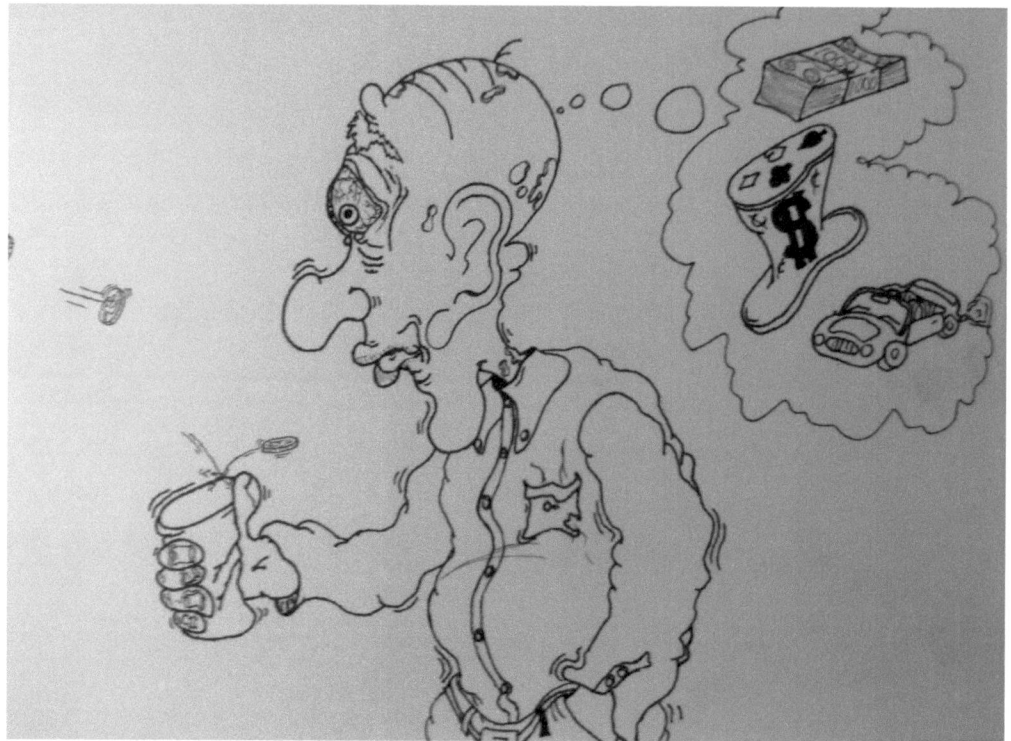

Change, Dream Big   1989   6 inches x 9 inches

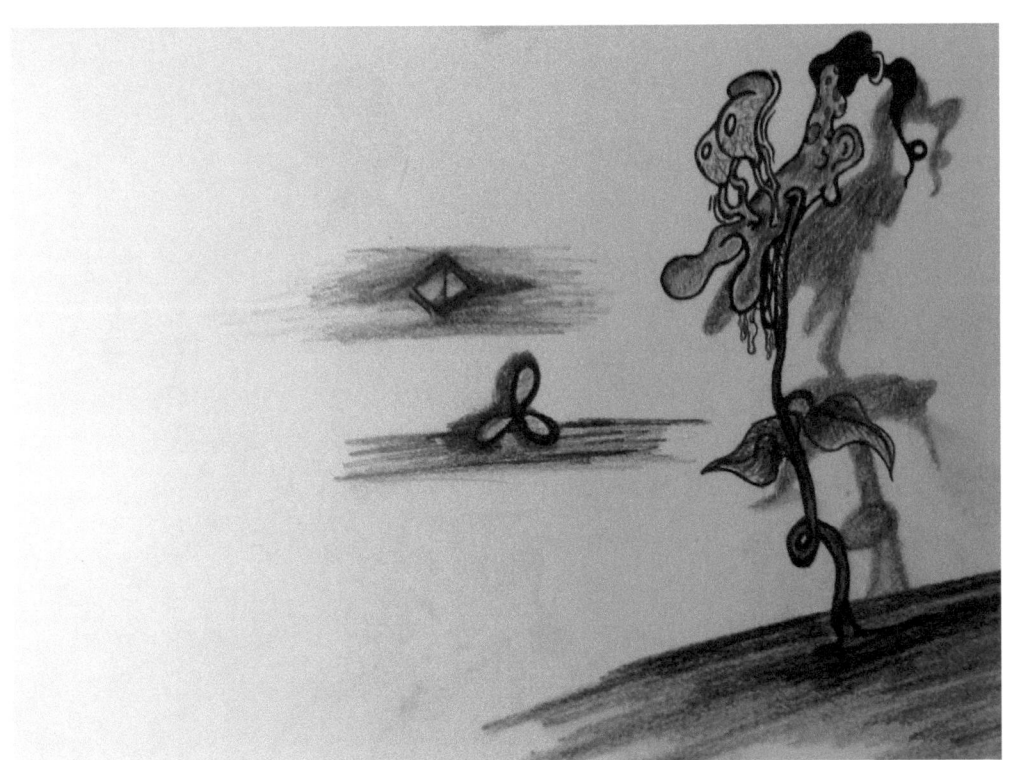

Pinhead Sprout   1990   6 inches x 6 inches

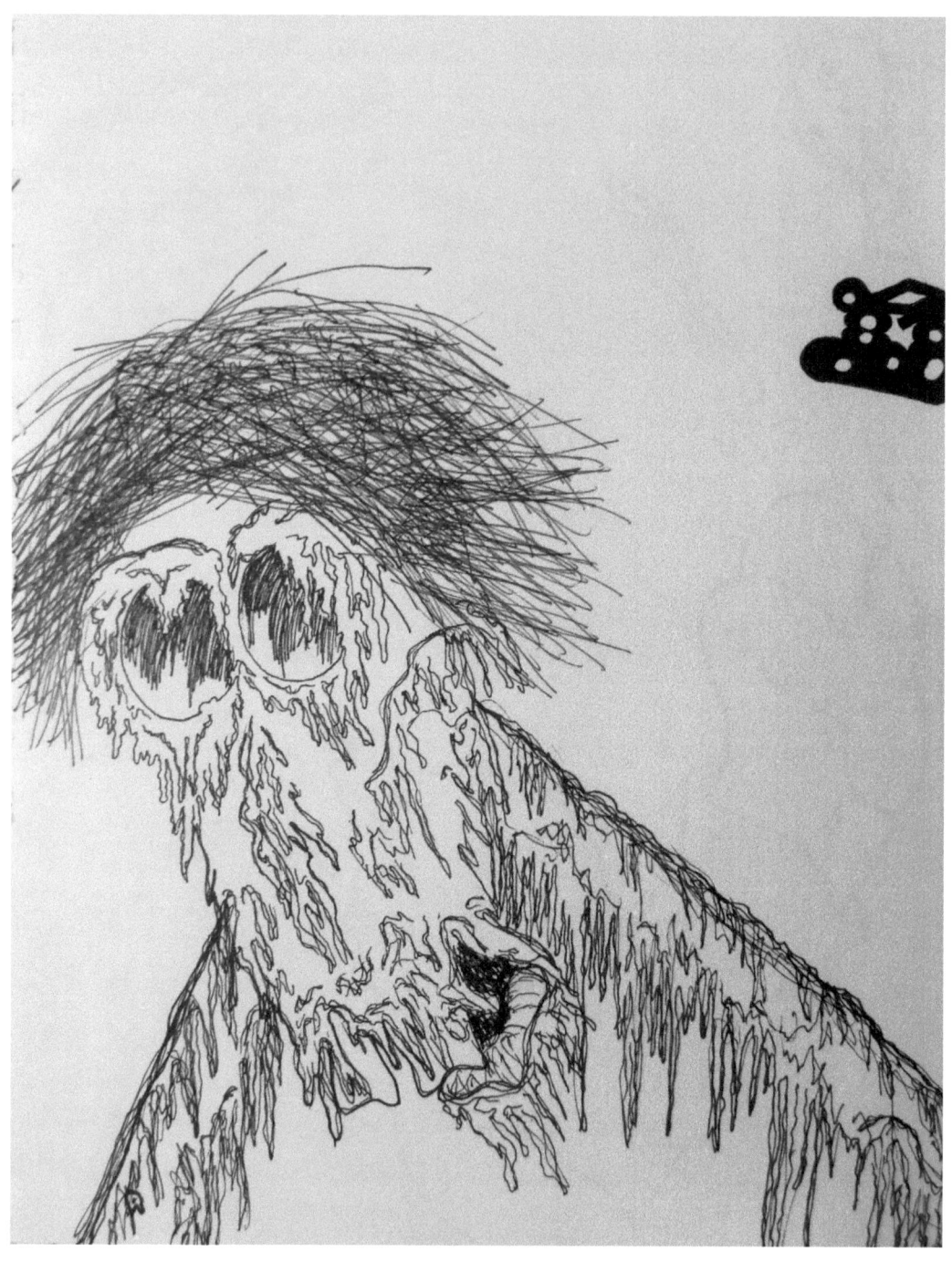

Some Kind of Evil   1990   6 inches x 7 inches

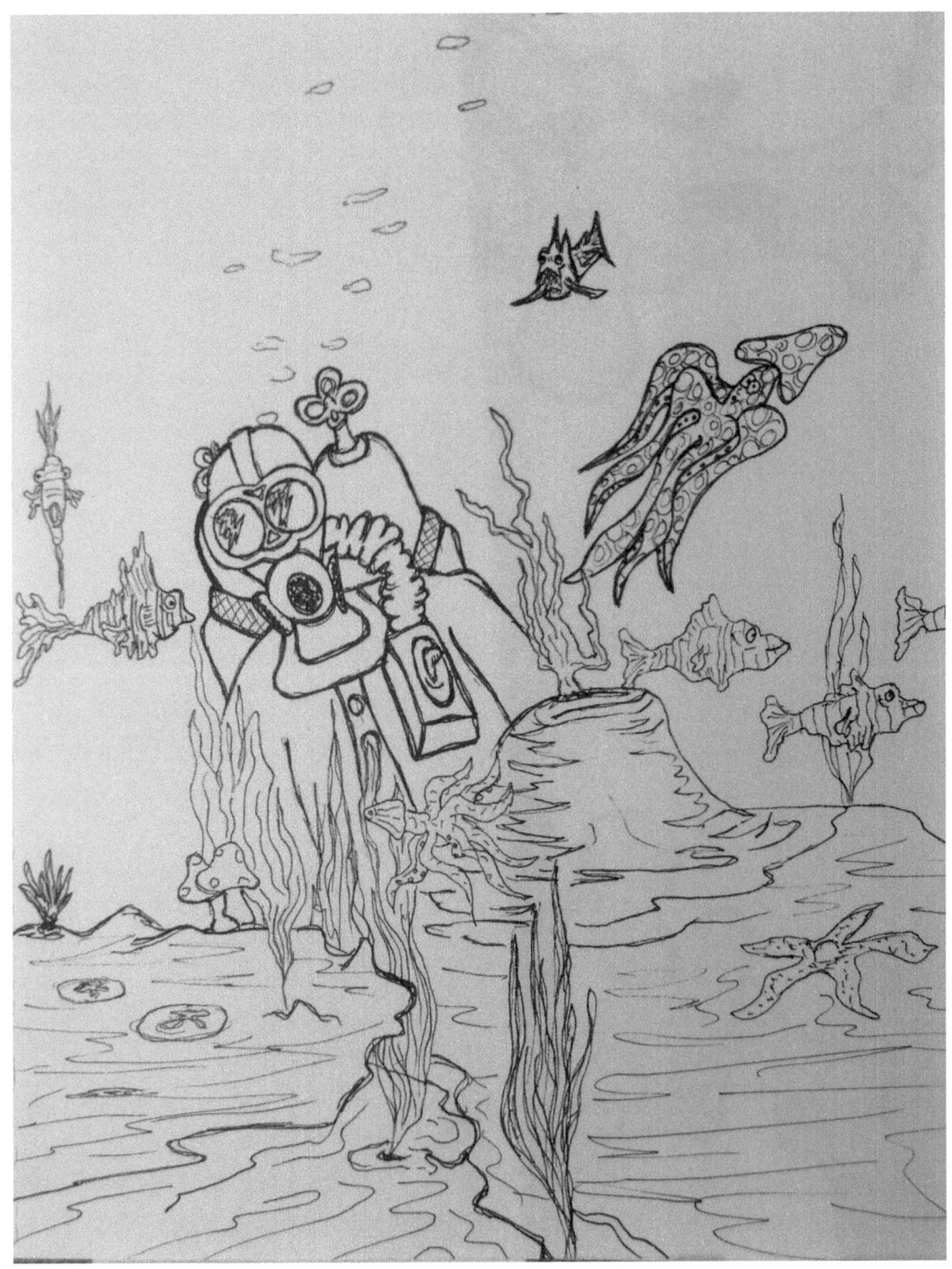

Sea Scape   1991   6 inches x 10 inches

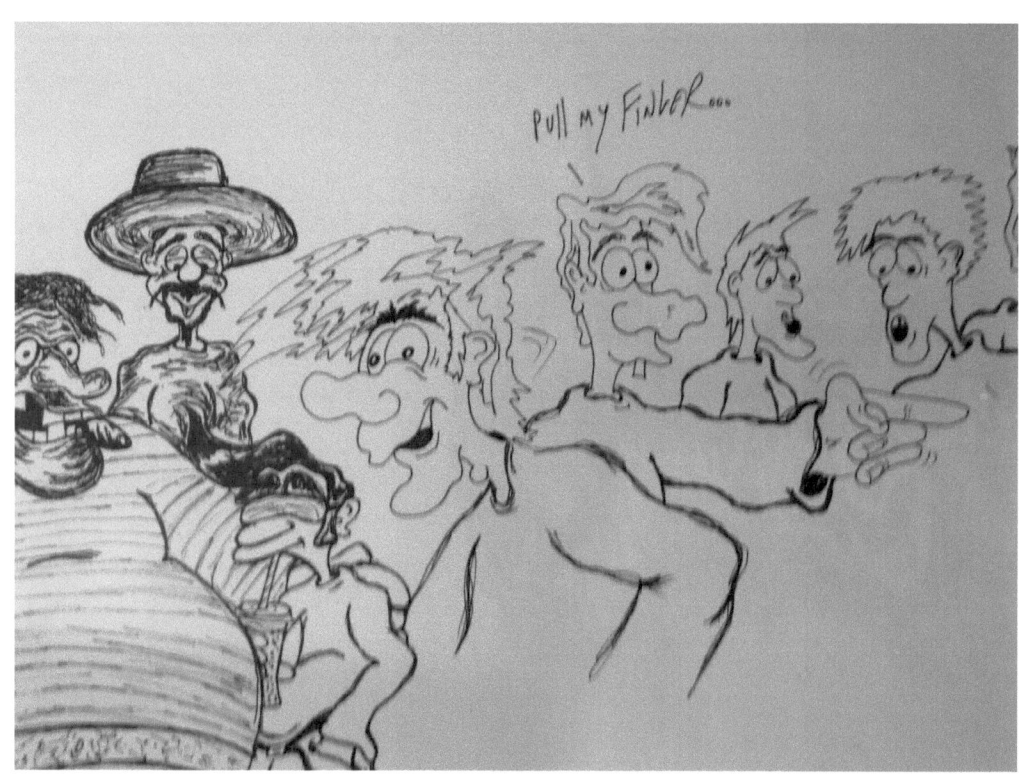

Pull My Finger   1992   10 inches x 6 inches

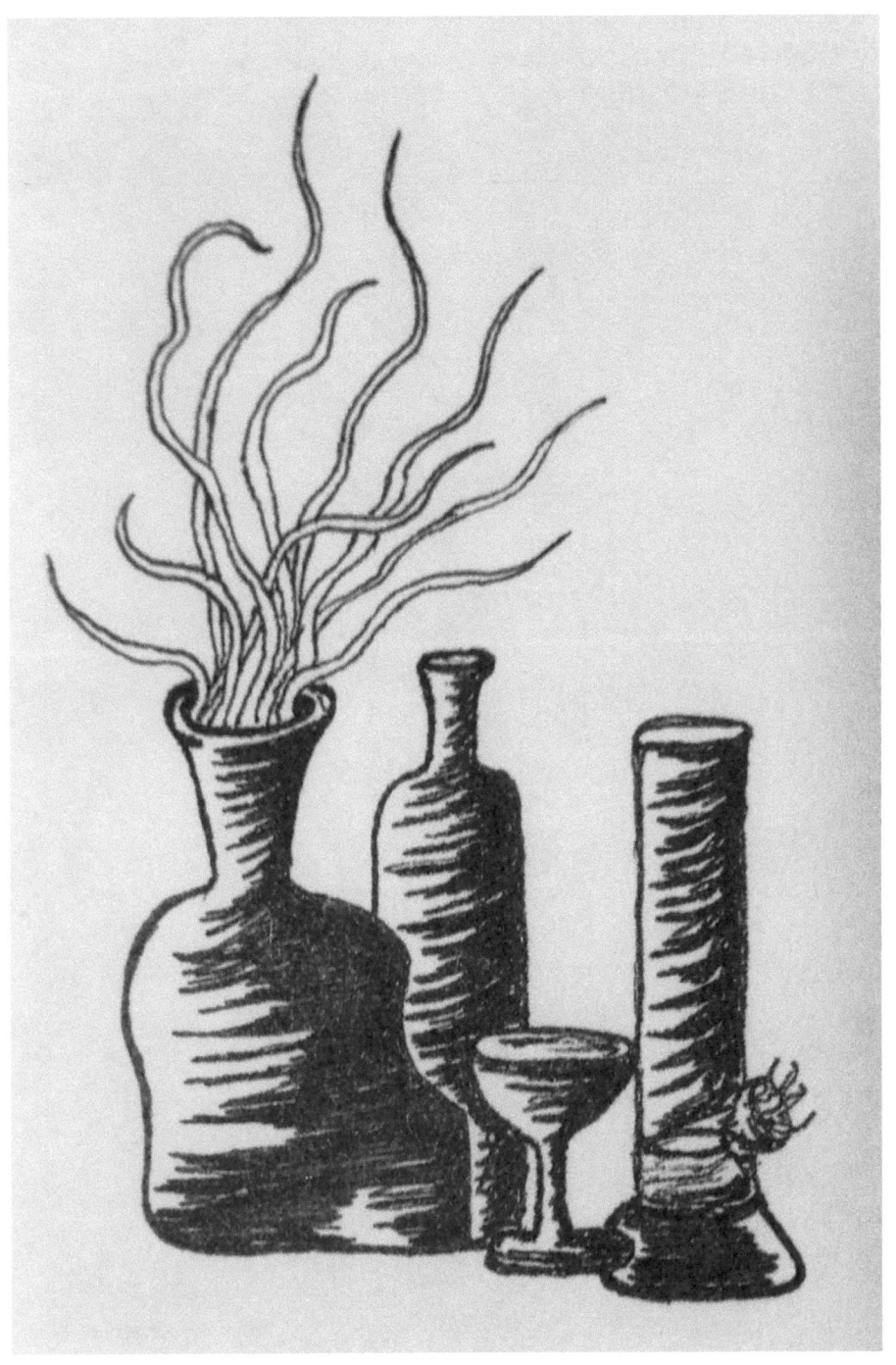

Glass Peace				1993		4 inches x 4 inches

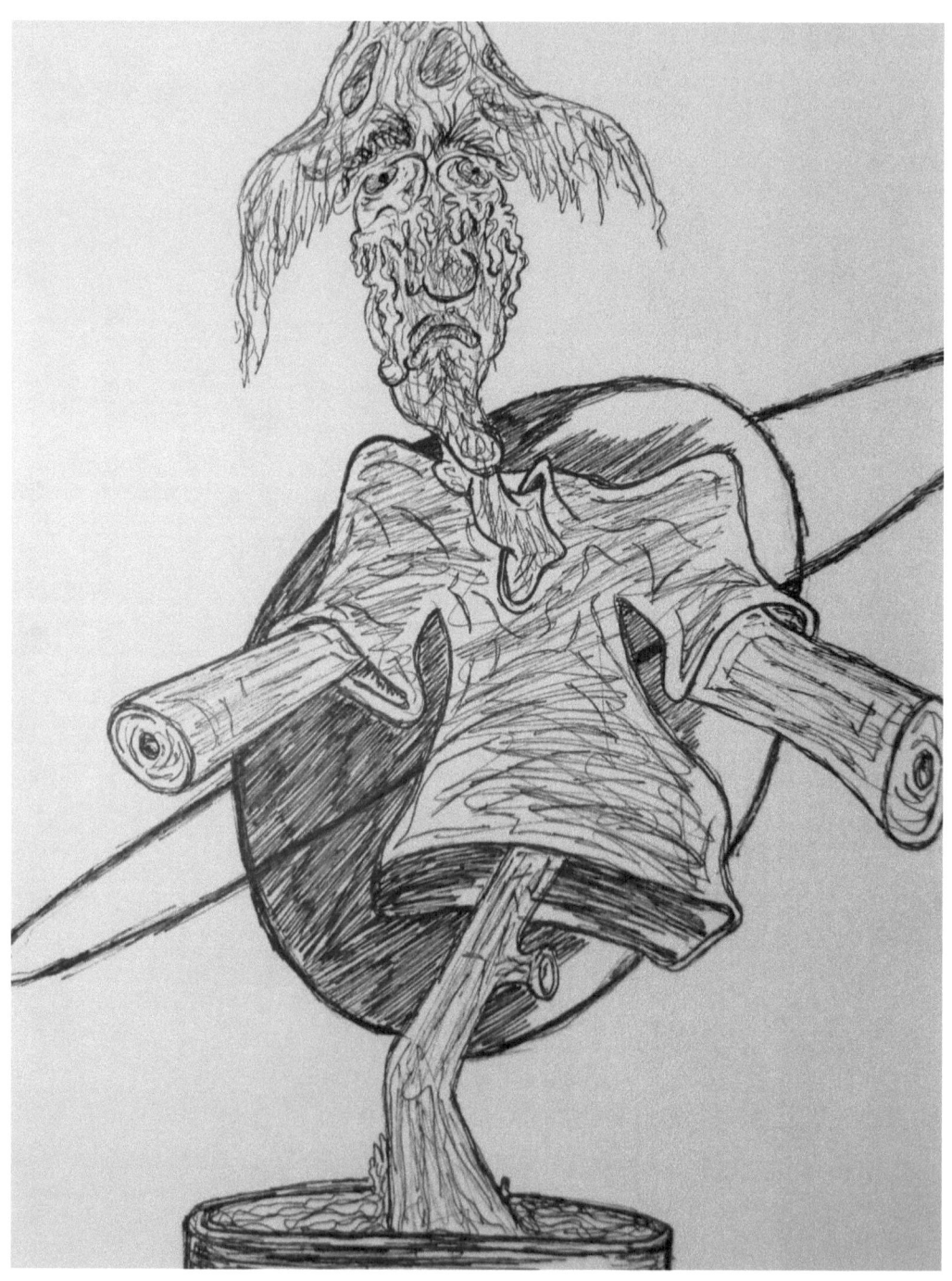

Space Plant Harvest Moon   1993   6 inches x 11 inches

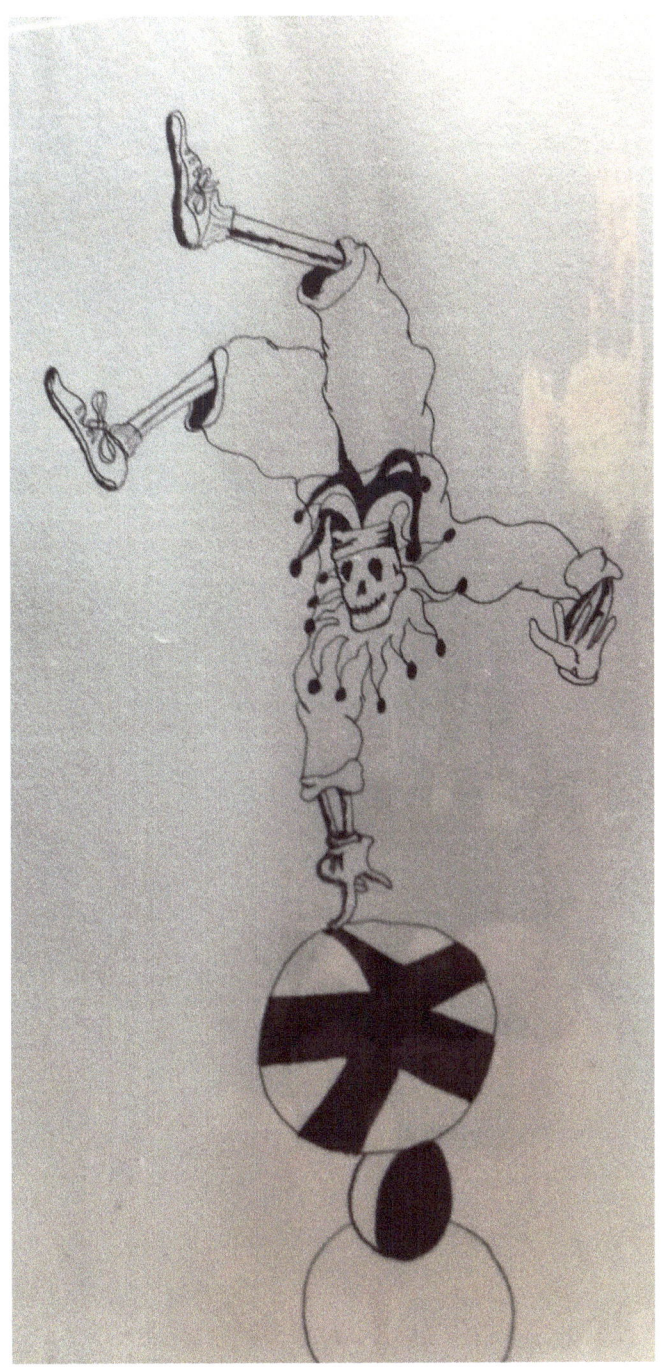

Jester Balance — 1993 — 4 inches x 10 inches

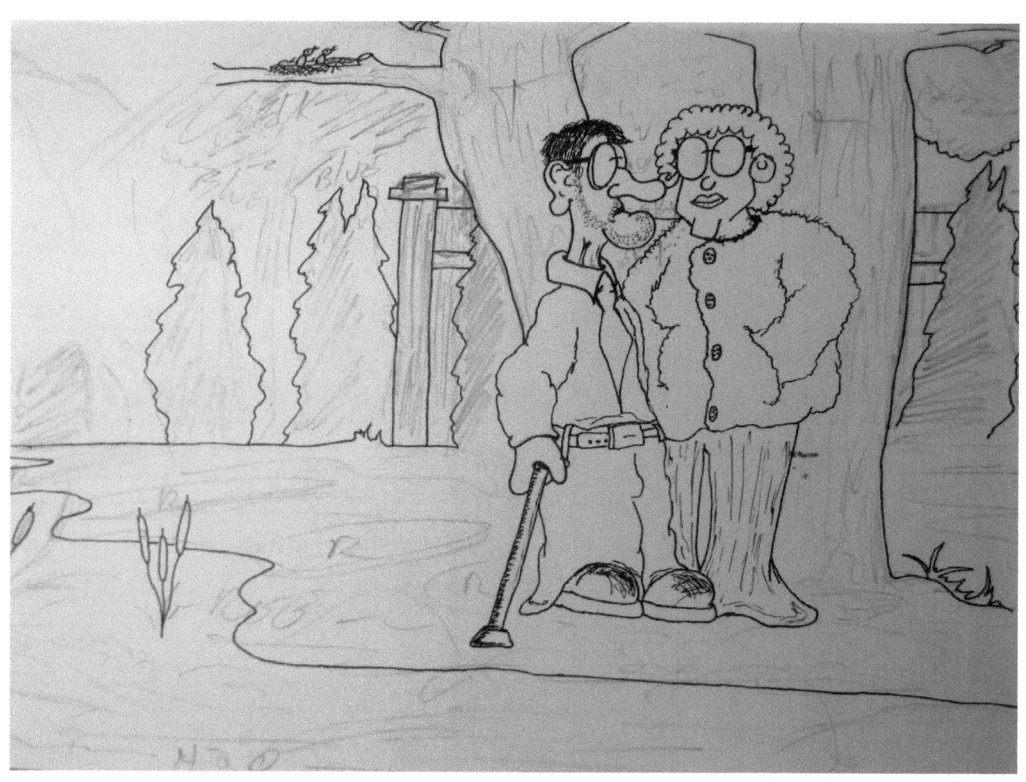

Unfinished Lovers — 1993 — 8 inches x 11 inches

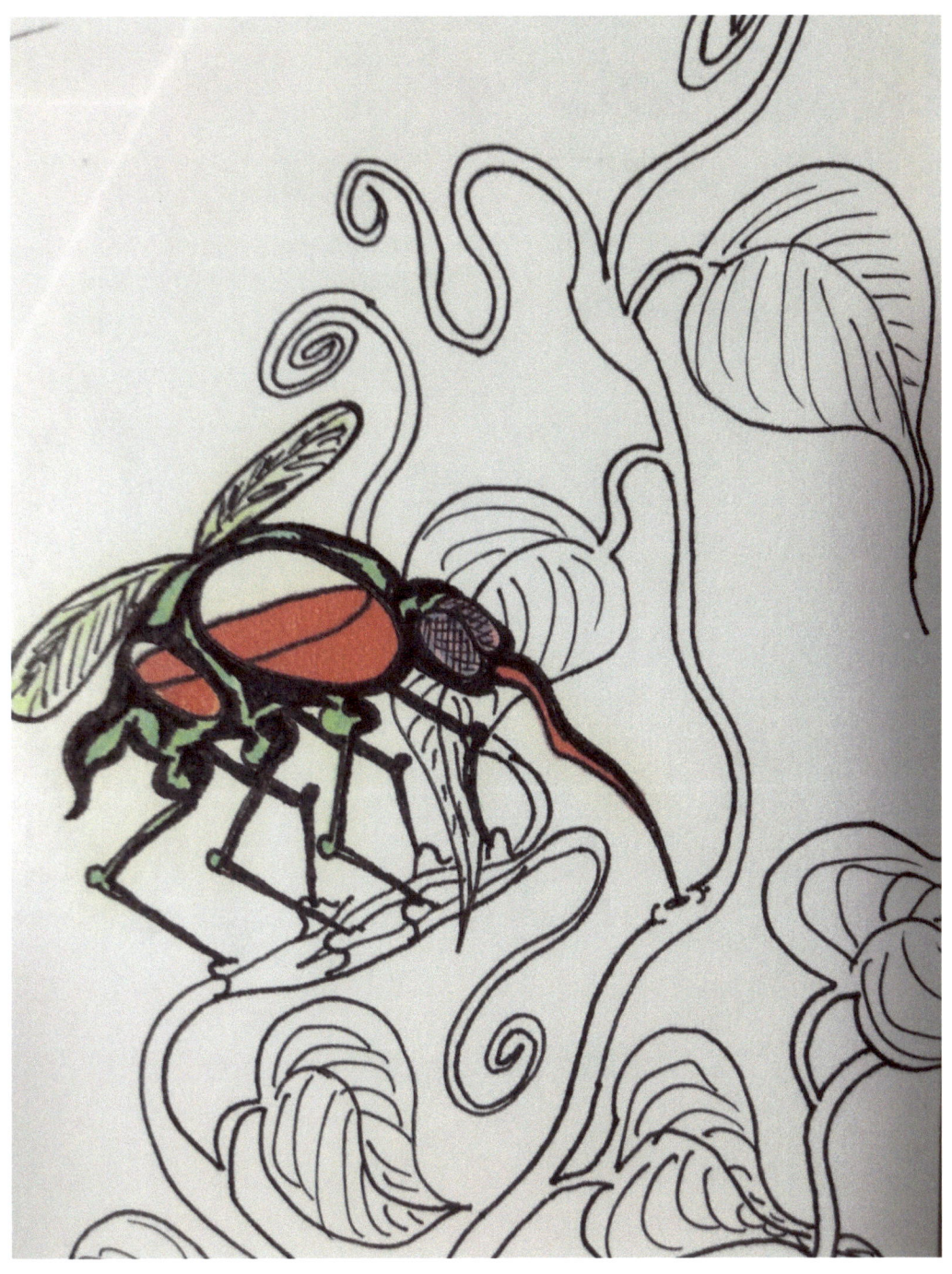

Life Sucker — 1994 — 5 inches x 7 inches

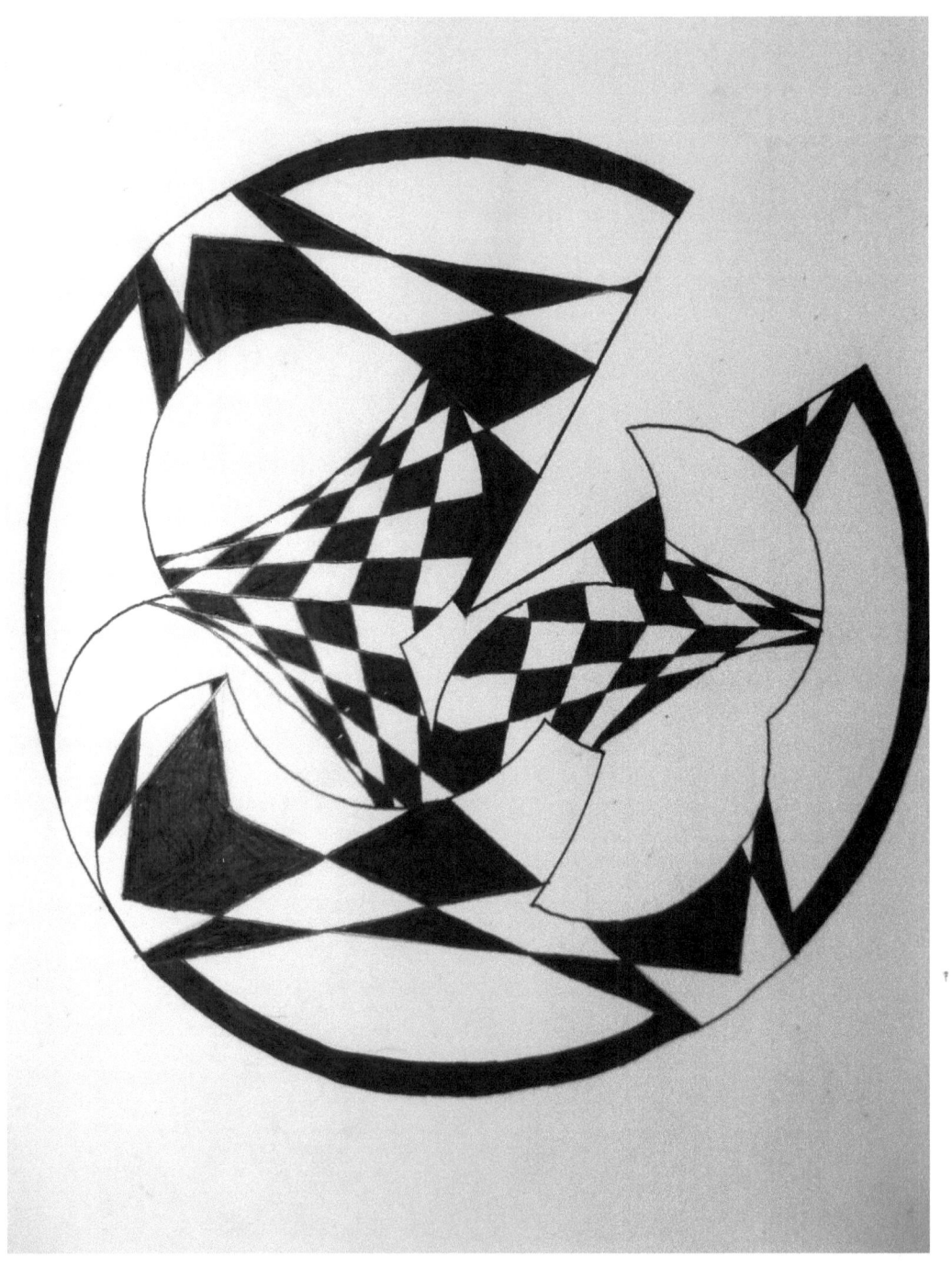

Distortion Sphere — 1994 — 8 inches x 8 inches

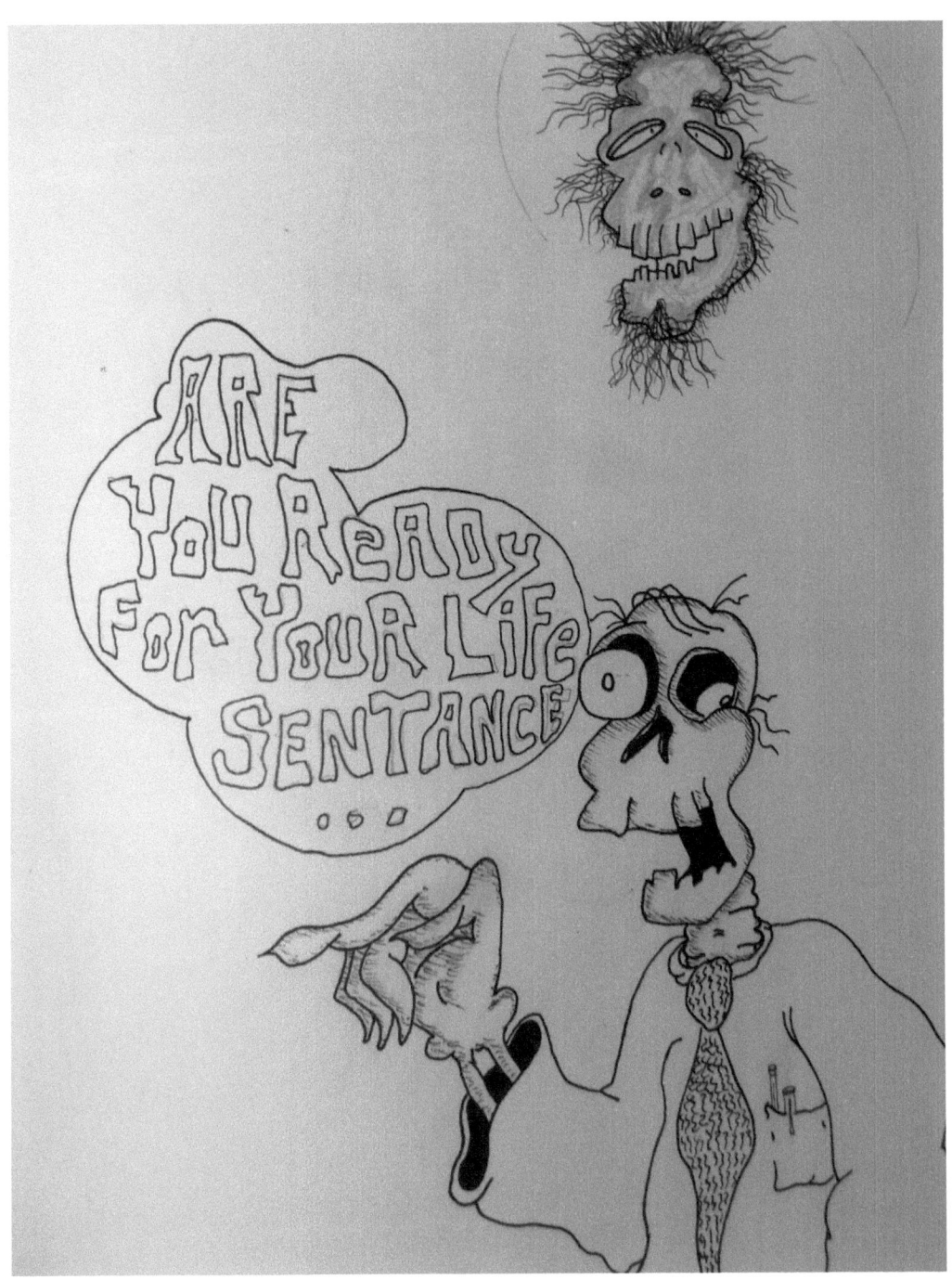

Graduation Only Weeks Away — 1994 — 8 inches x 11 inches

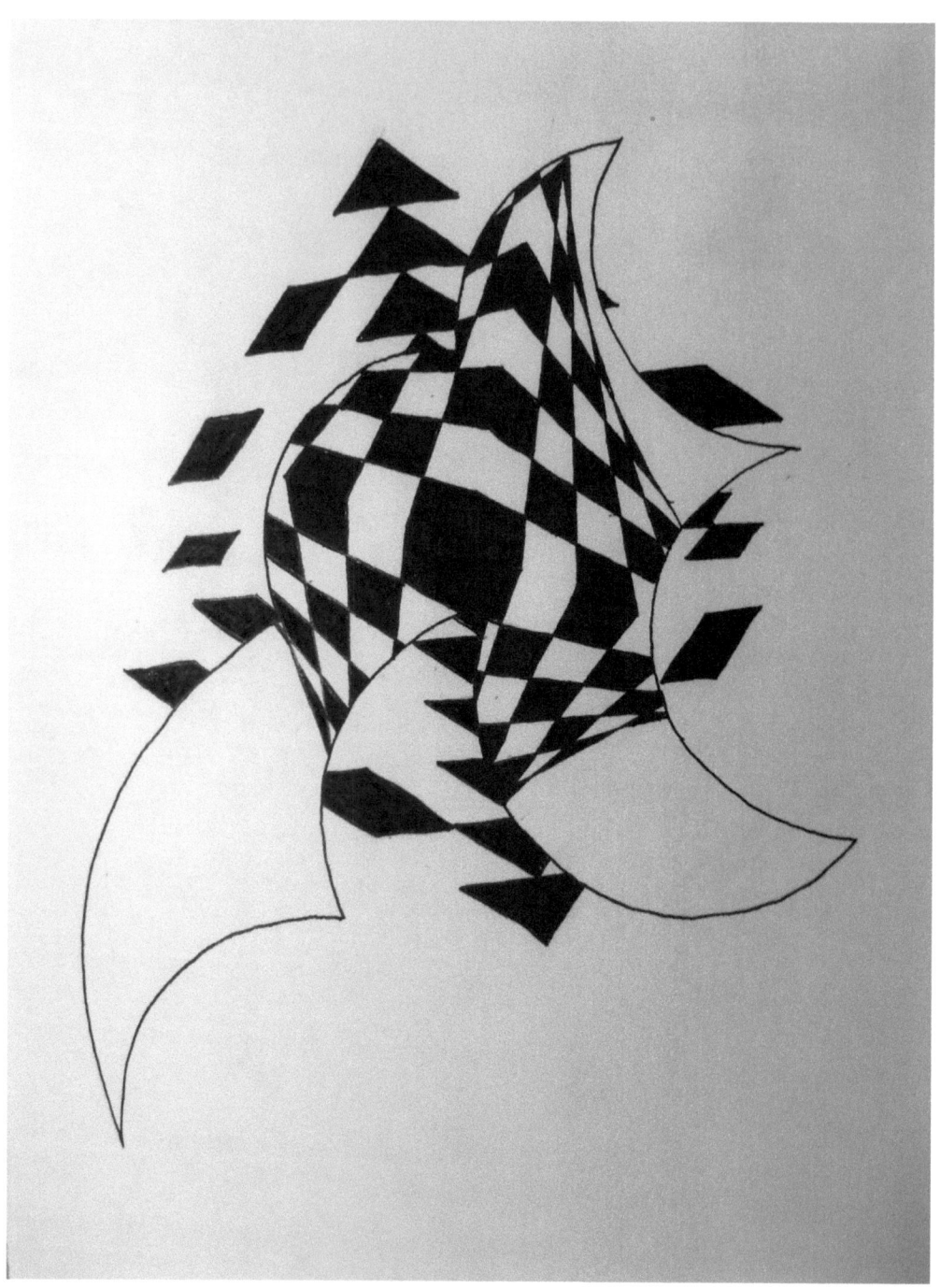

Checkered Board   1994   7 inches x 8 inches

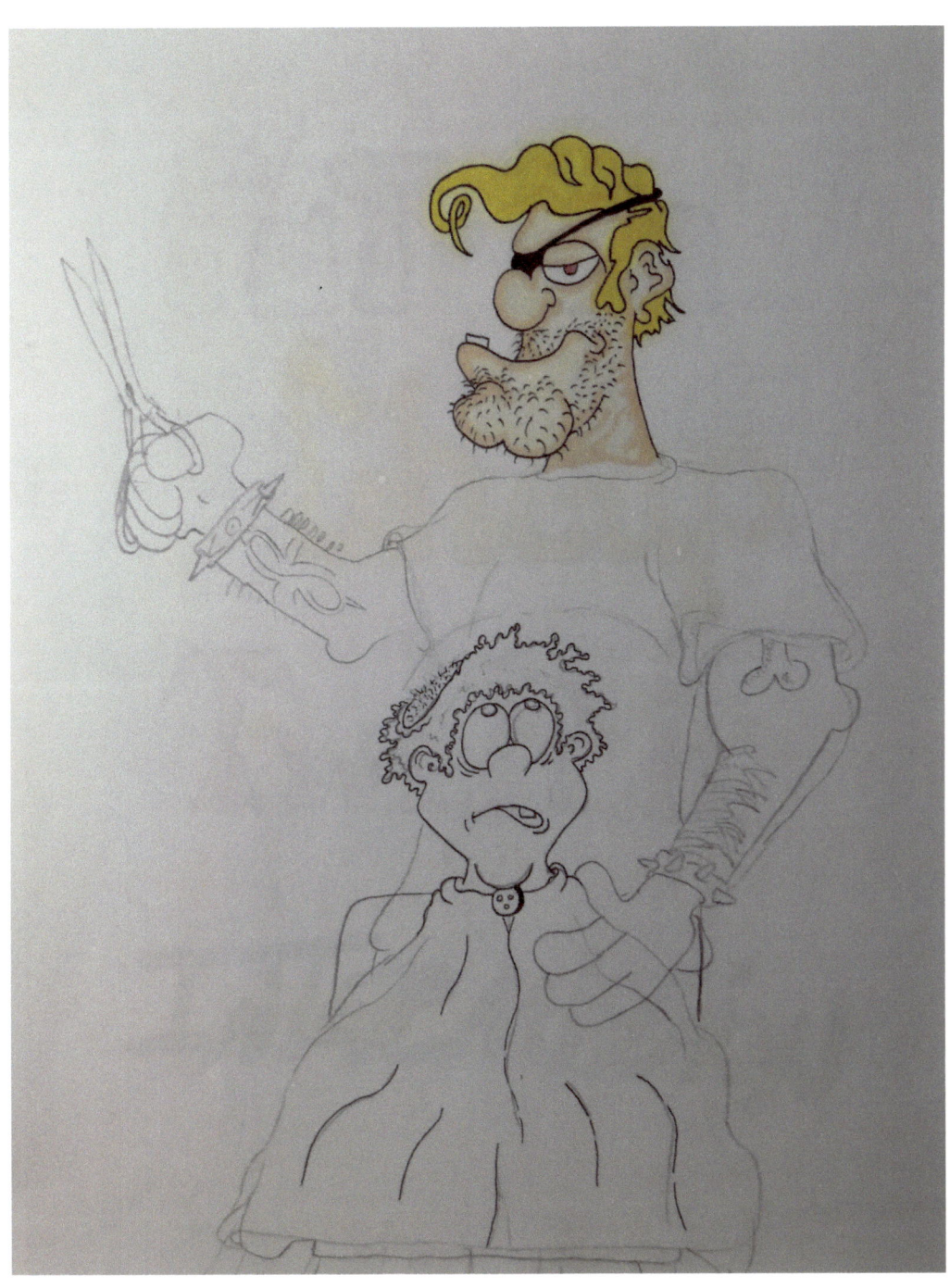

Unfinished Hair Chop   1994   7 inches x 10 inches

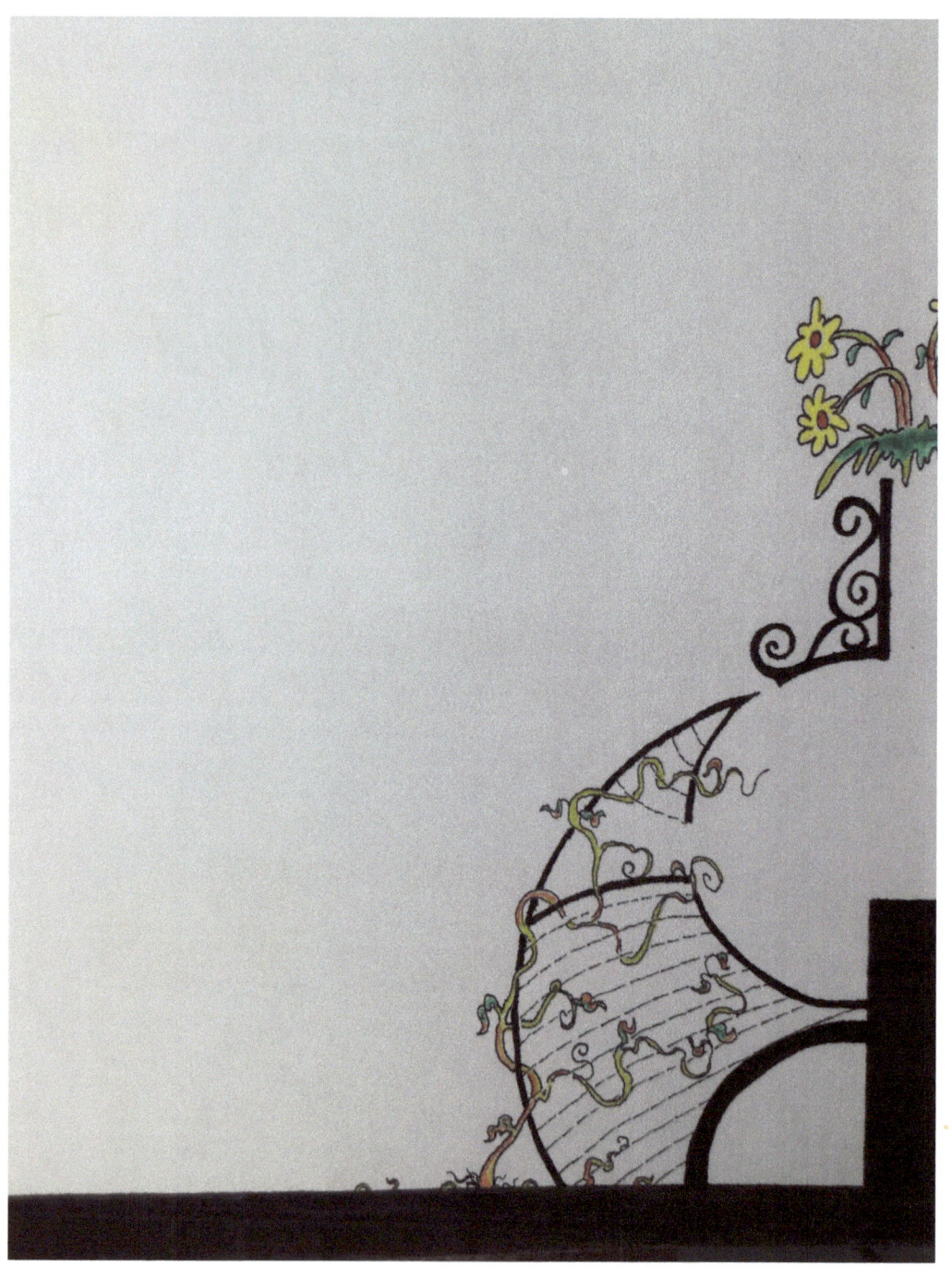

Breece Tries to Draw   1994   7 inches x 7 inches

Only a few weeks after high school graduation attending college away from home. Listening to college professors during those perfect Summer mornings. So much freedom with so many restrictions.

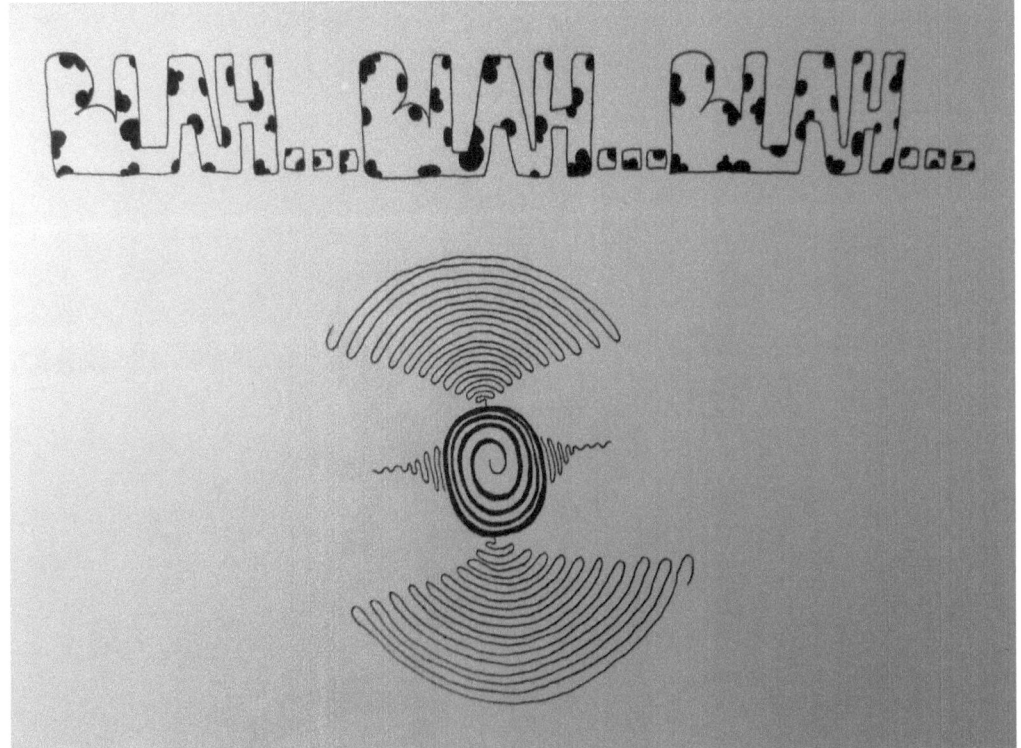

Blah…Blah…Blah…   1994   8 inches x 7 inches

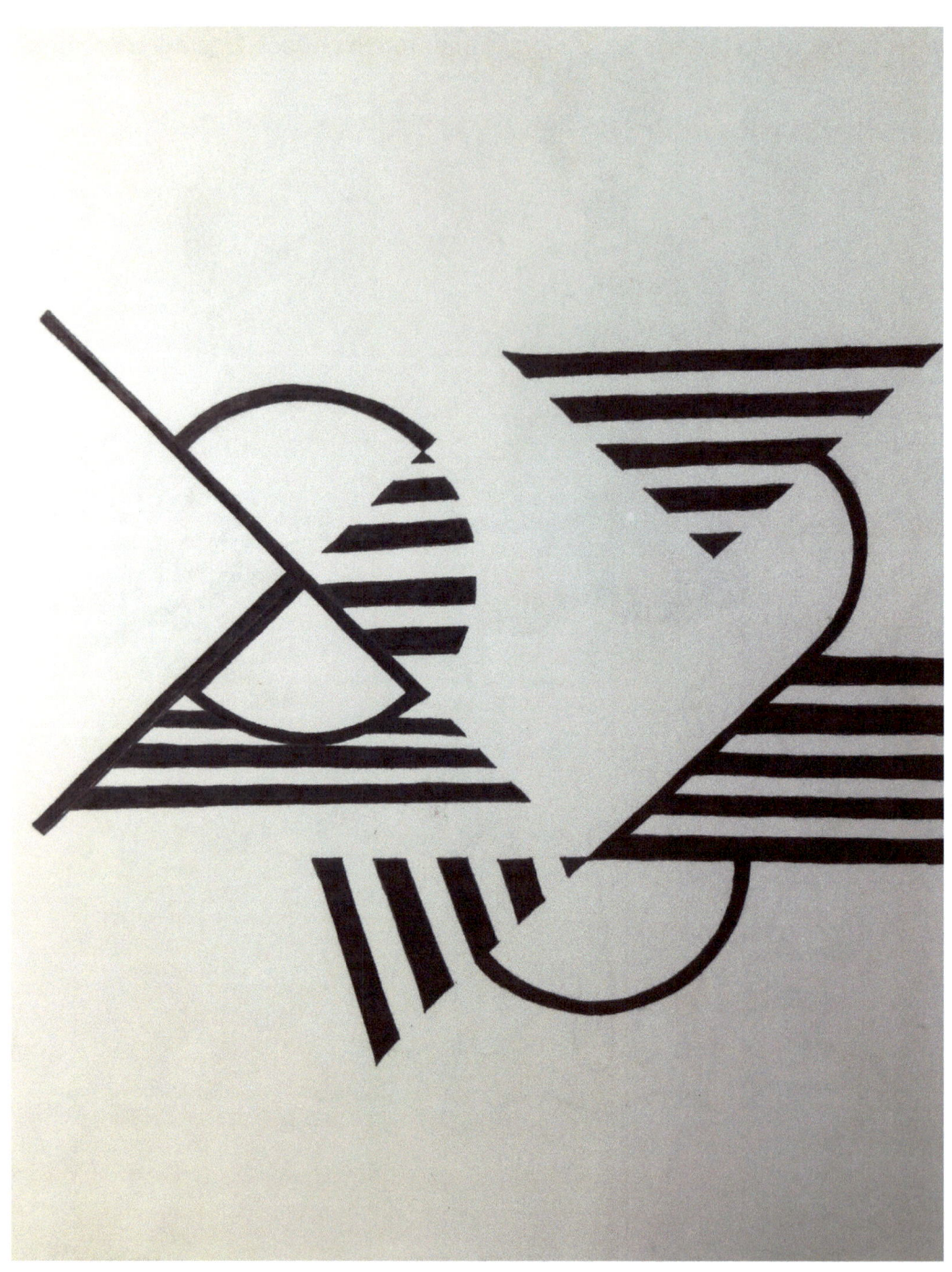

Lines Over Shapes		1994		9 inches x 7 inches

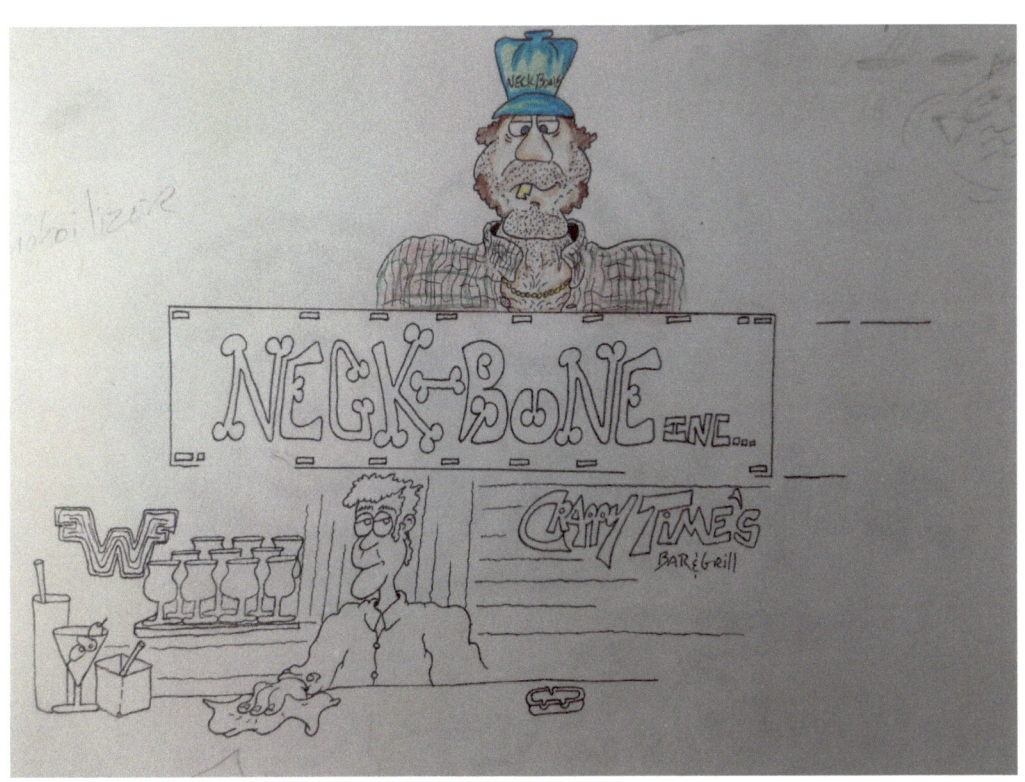

Neck Bone the Trucker   1994   8 inches x 7 inches

Some travels out west and then many more traveling adventures. Not many cameras choices in the 1990's. Most were taken with my reliable Pentax 35 mm used for black and white photos or a disposable 35mm used for color. The disposable cameras were usually damaged or lost before photos developed. I recalled this billboard somewhere out there in the desert, so out of place. So I drew it.

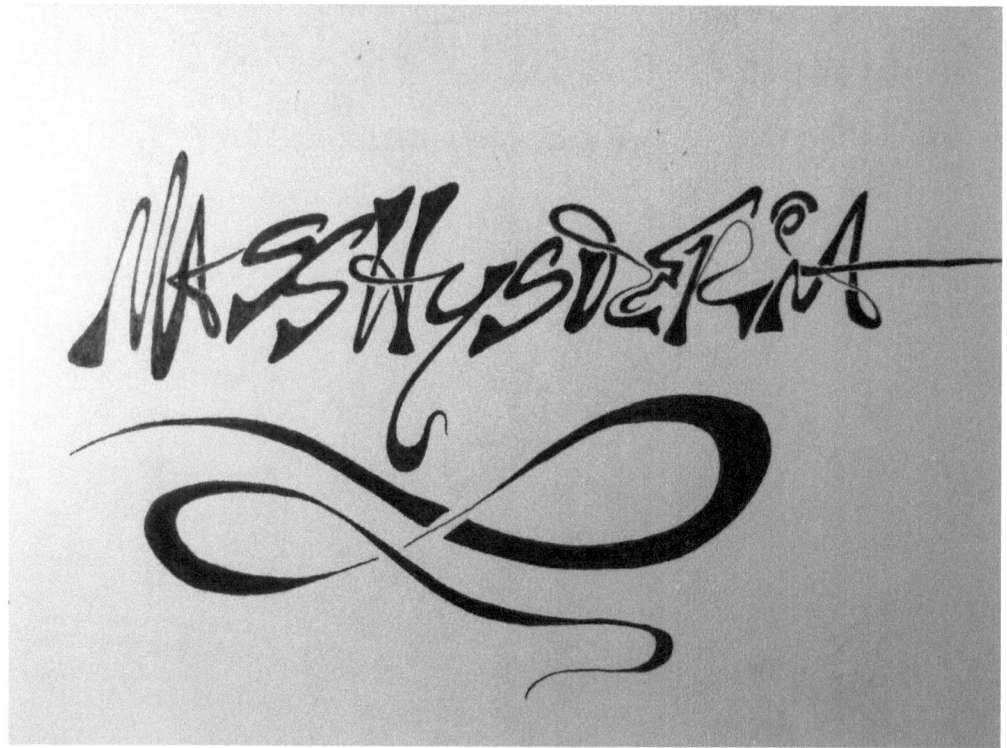

Billboard in Phoenix   1996   7 inches x 4 inches

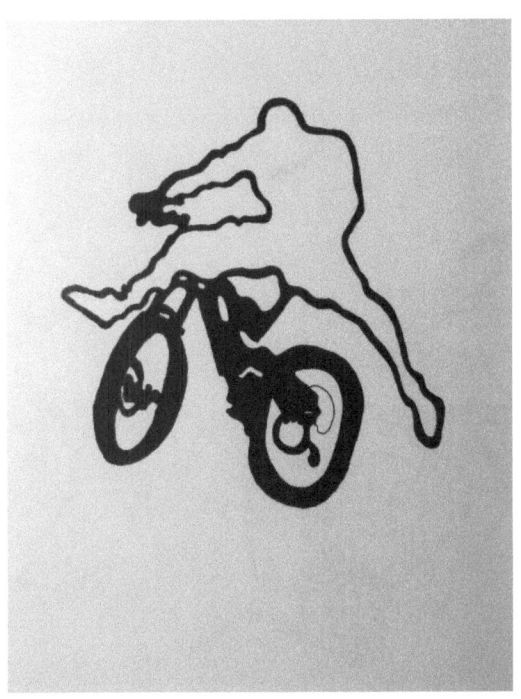

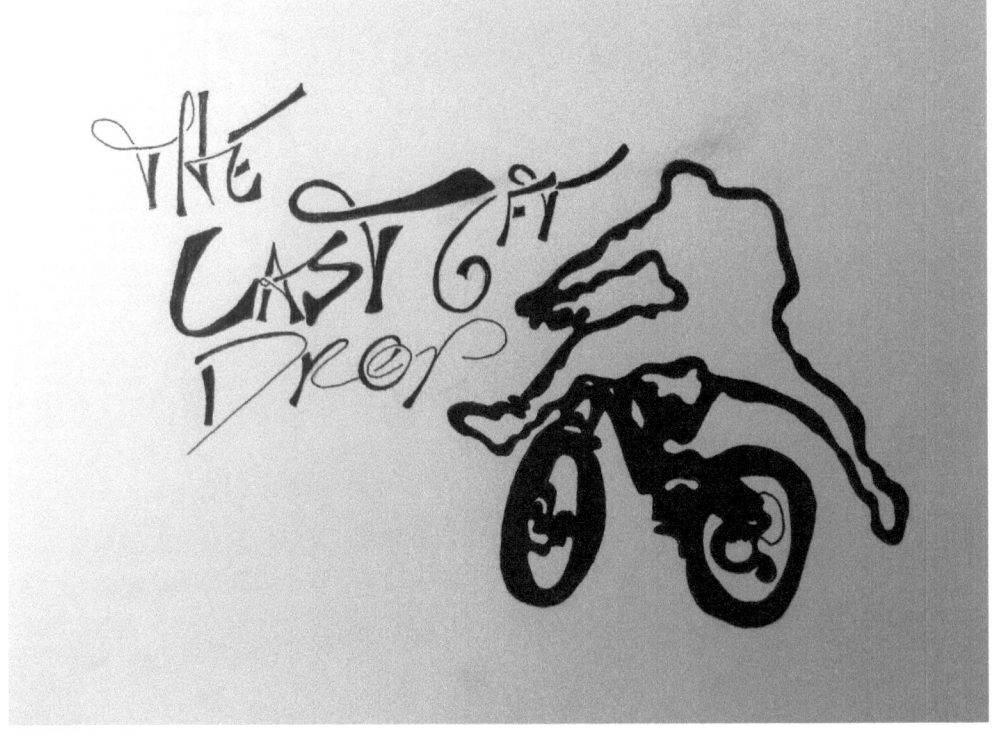

Cronomer (top)   2001   4 inches x 4 inches
Drop Dead (bottom)   2001   9 inches x 6 inches

Kingsford my pet snake was a part of my life from 2003 until 2014.

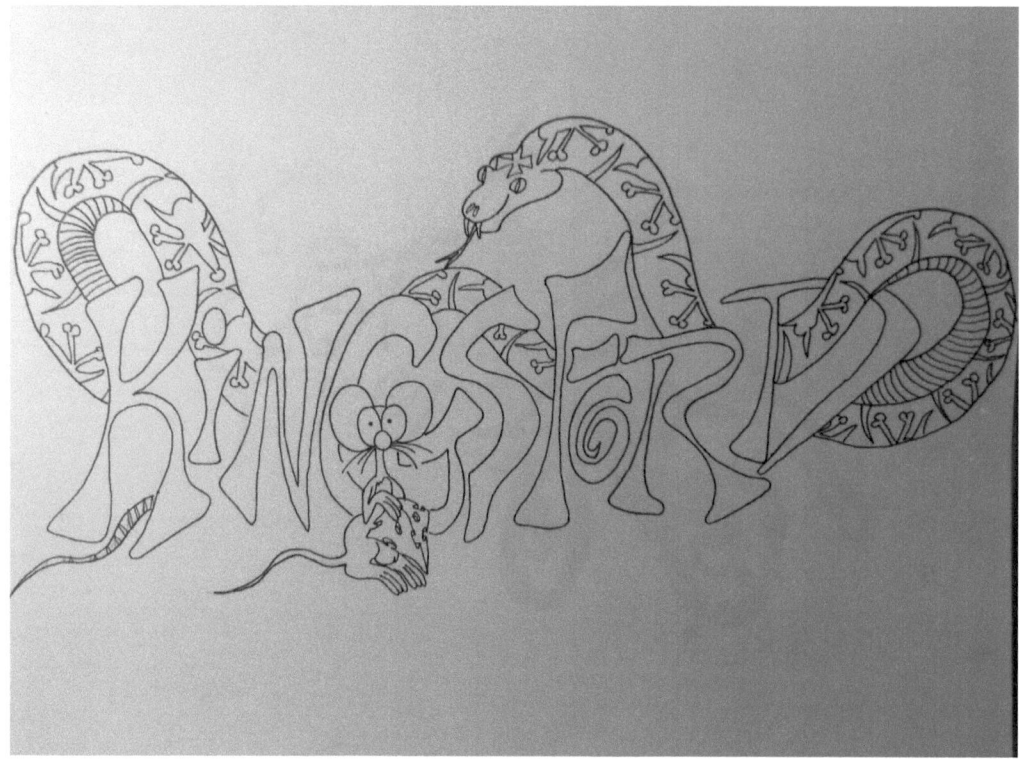

Charcoal Corn Snake   2003   10 inches x 6 inches

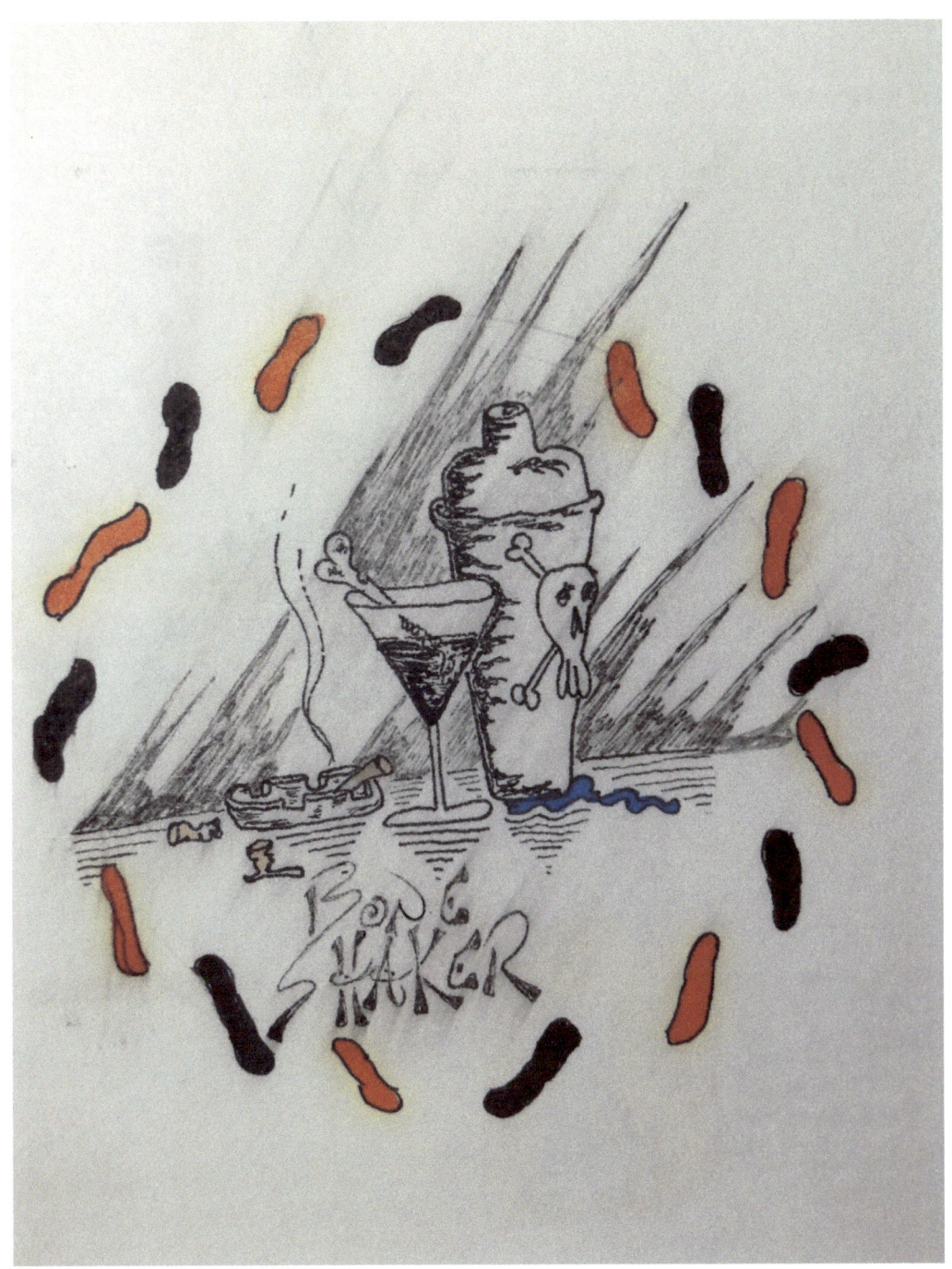

Bone Shaker and Martini   2004   4 inches x 4 inches

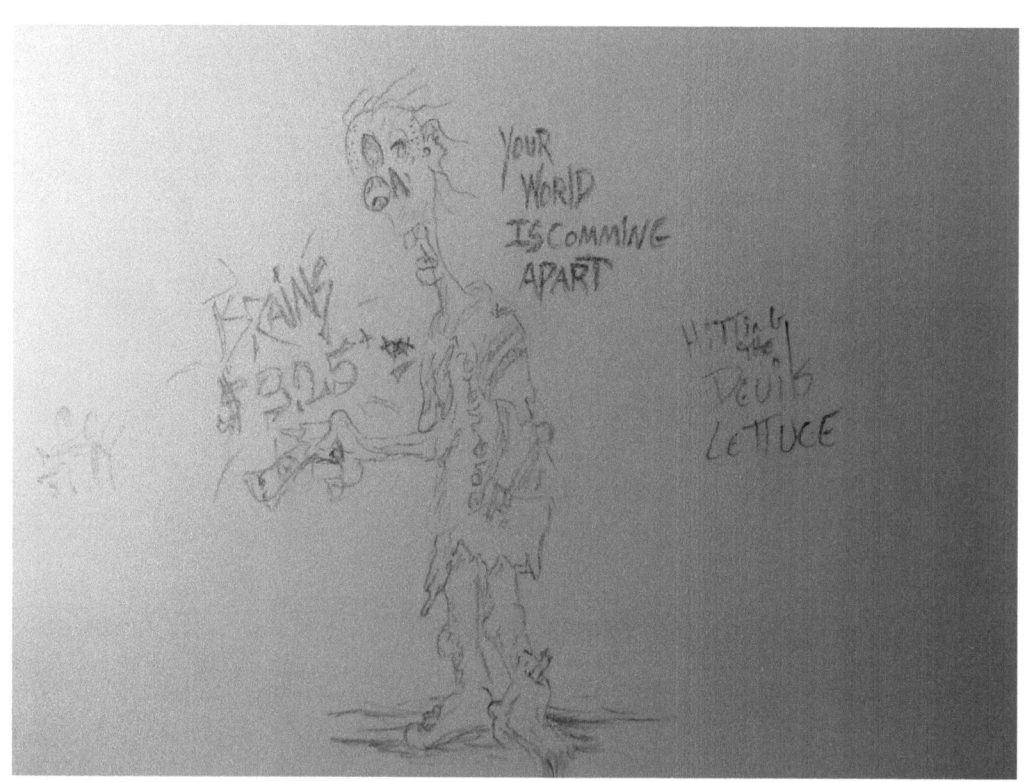

Unfinished Brains on Sale   2010   8 inches x 8 inches

I spent many years not drawing. My hands hurt from wrenching not to mention how dirty they got from motorcycles.

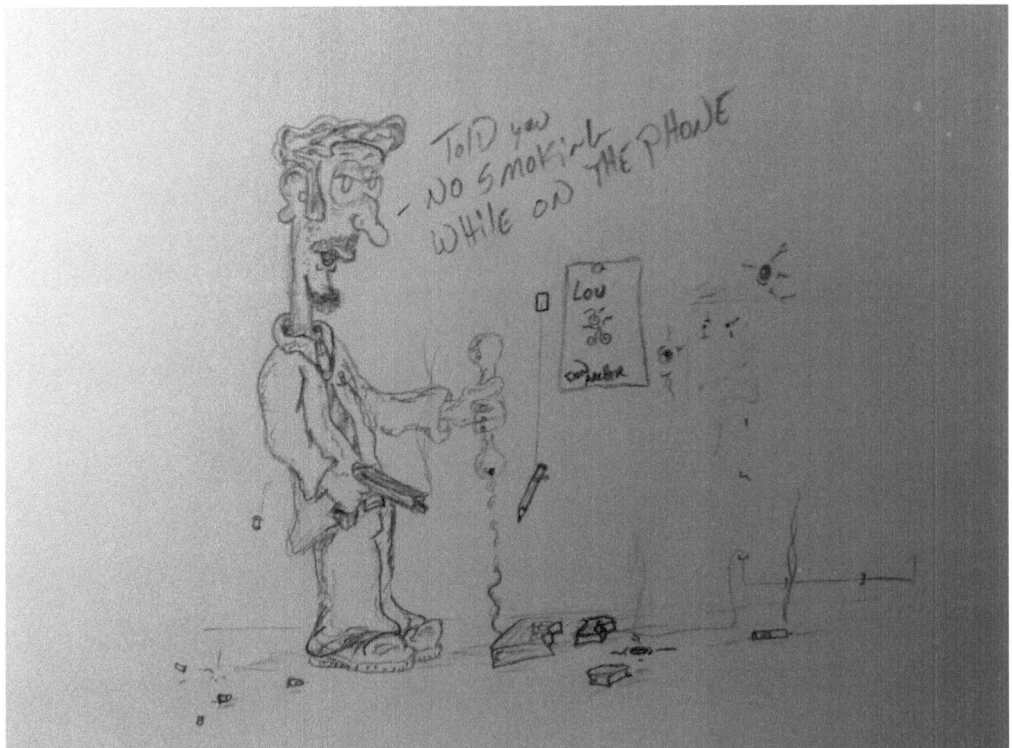

Unfinished Lou   2010   8 inches x 7 inches

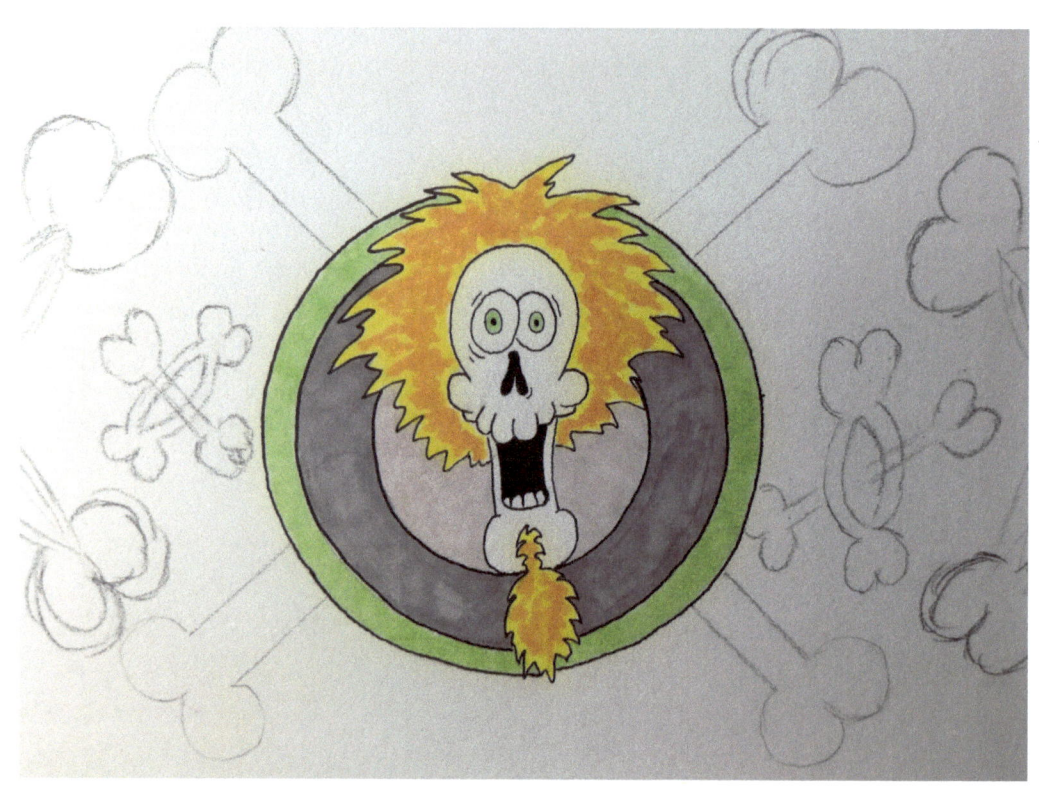

Unfinished Bone Face   2014   10 inches x 5 inches

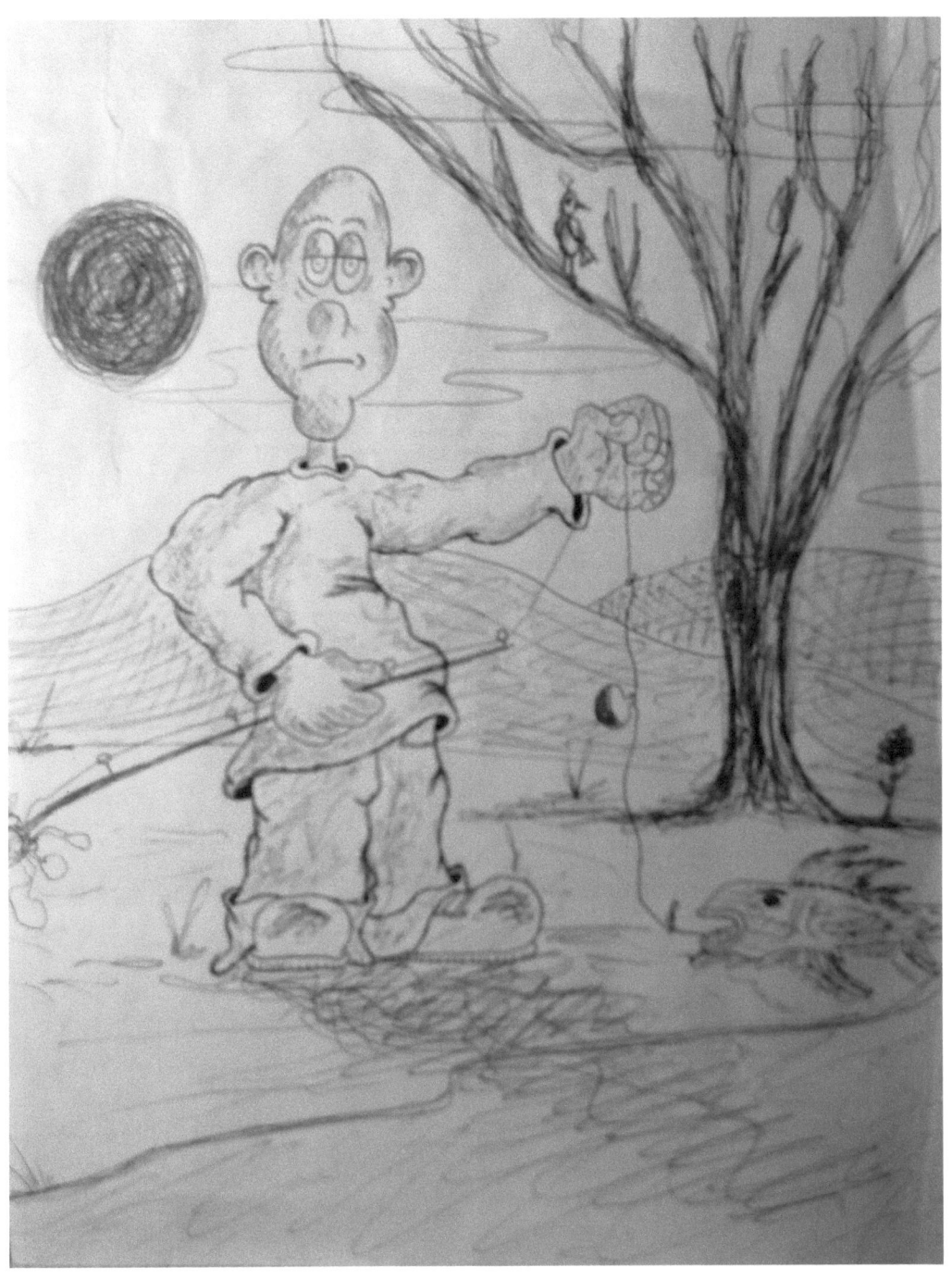

Drew this on the back of a NYDoL work search record sheet from years prior. Waiting for a set of keys to arrive. Key was in the ignition. Turning a negative situation into a positive one. After working for a days pay, I was unsuccessful trying to break into the vehicle so I had some time to sit, relax and draw.

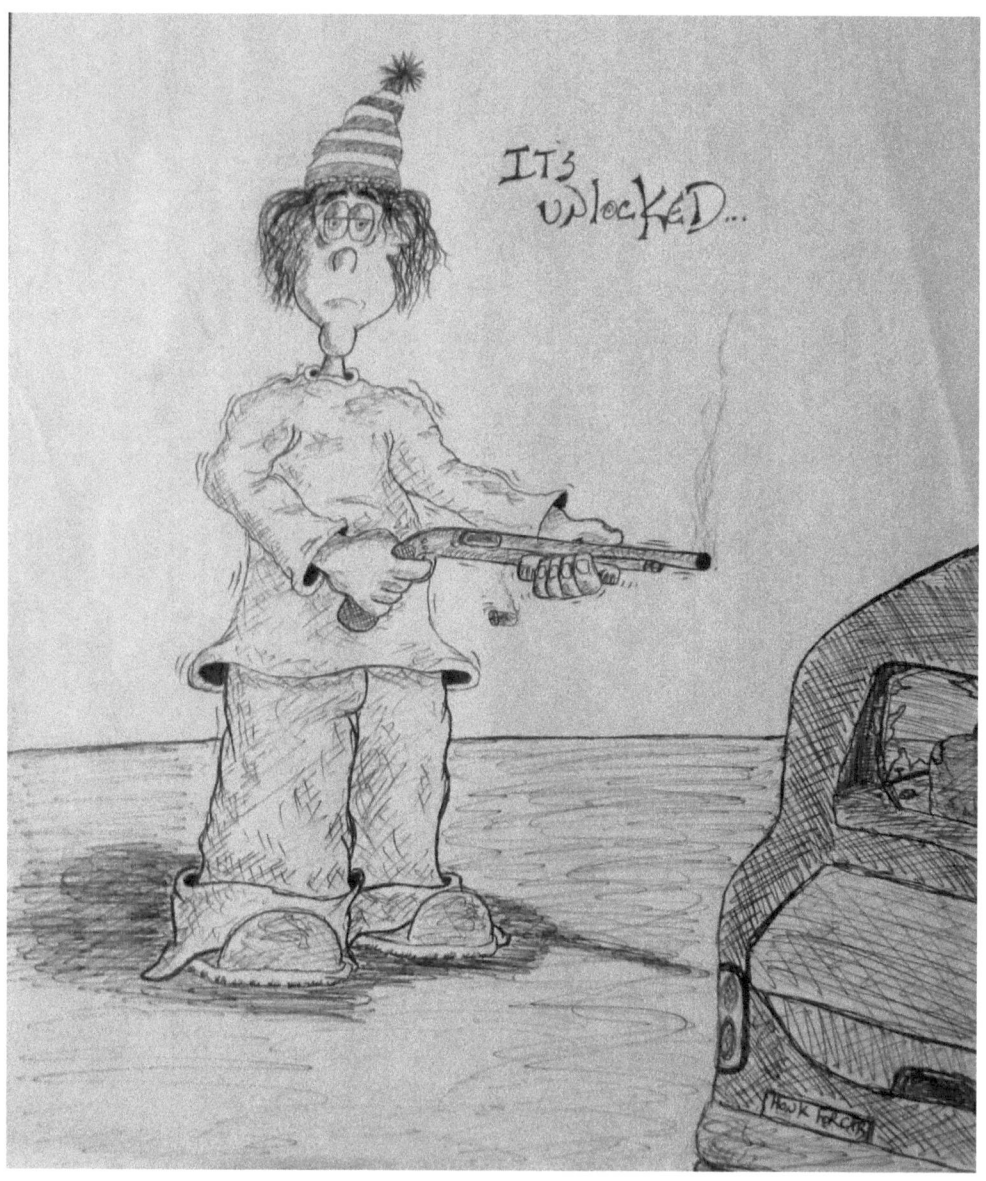

Locked Out Dept. of Labor   2016   11 inches x 8 inches

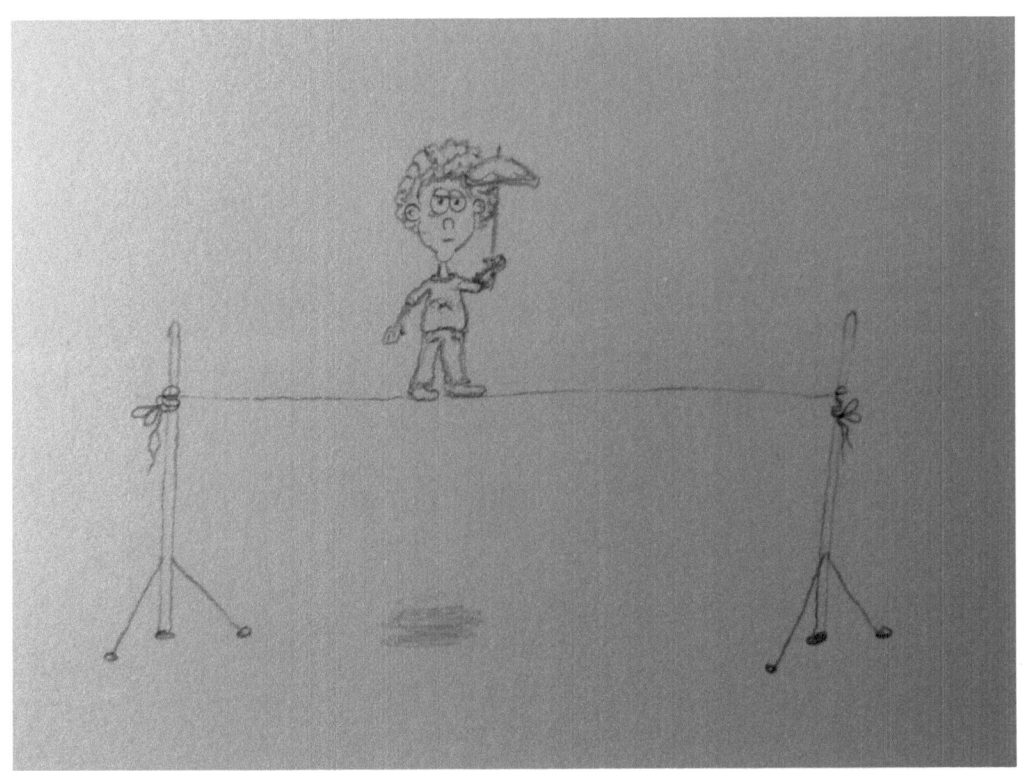

Tight Wired   2017   5 inches x 4 inches

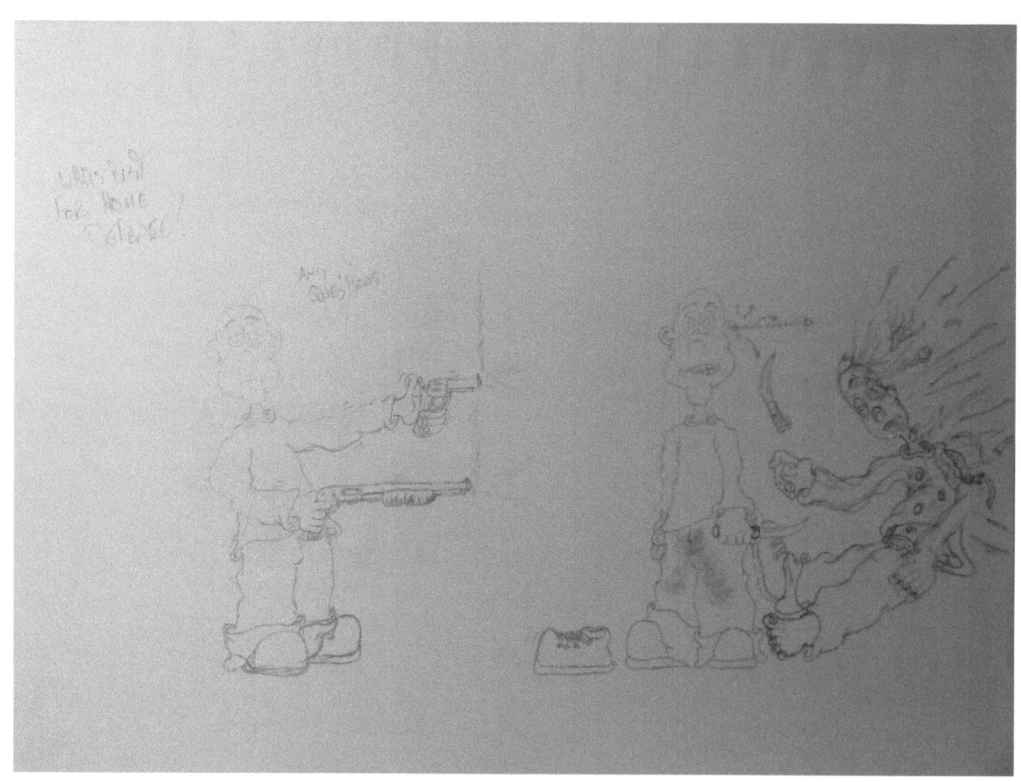

Unfinished Home Defense — 2018 — 14 inches x 11 inches

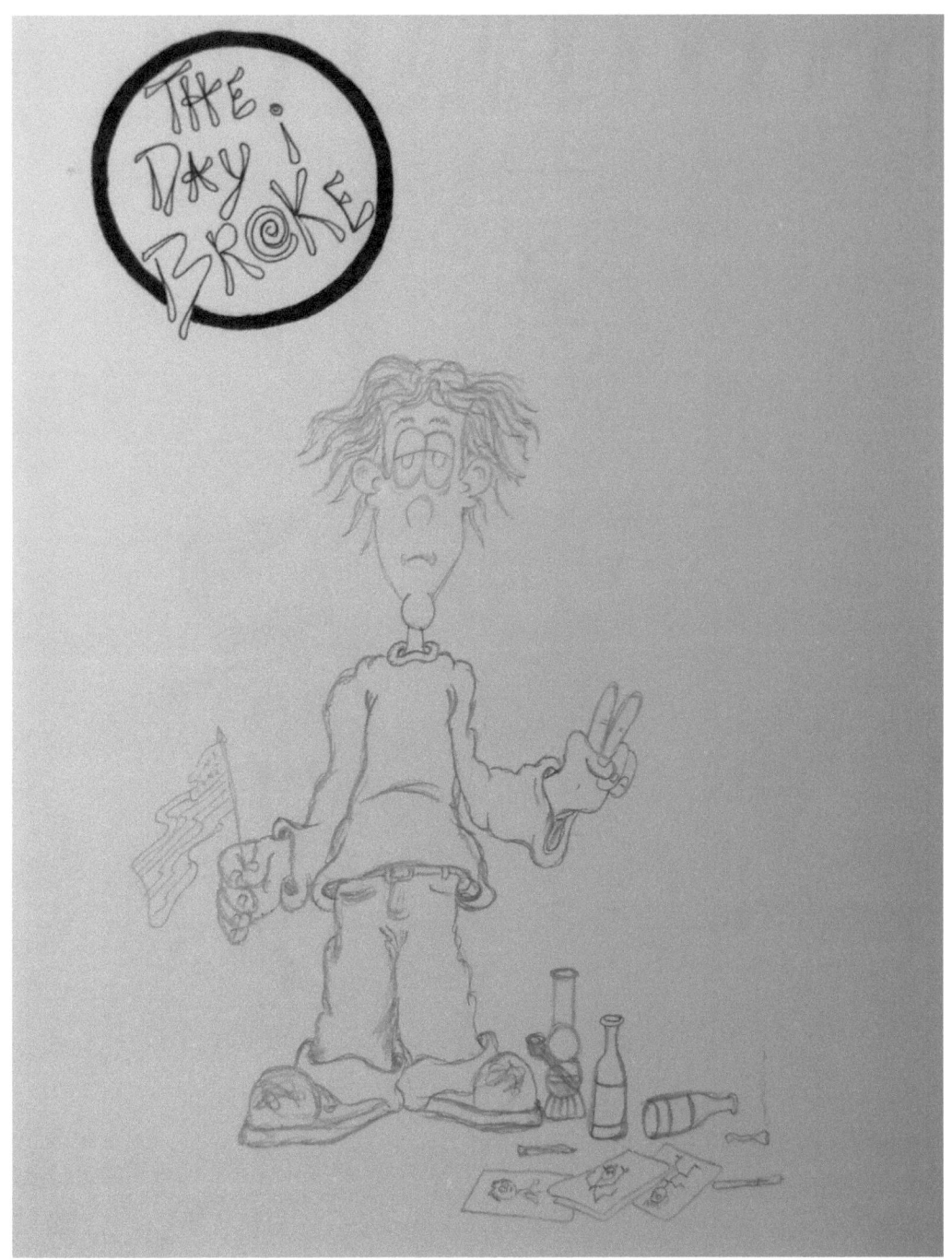

Unfinished The Day i Broke   2018   8 inches x 11 inches

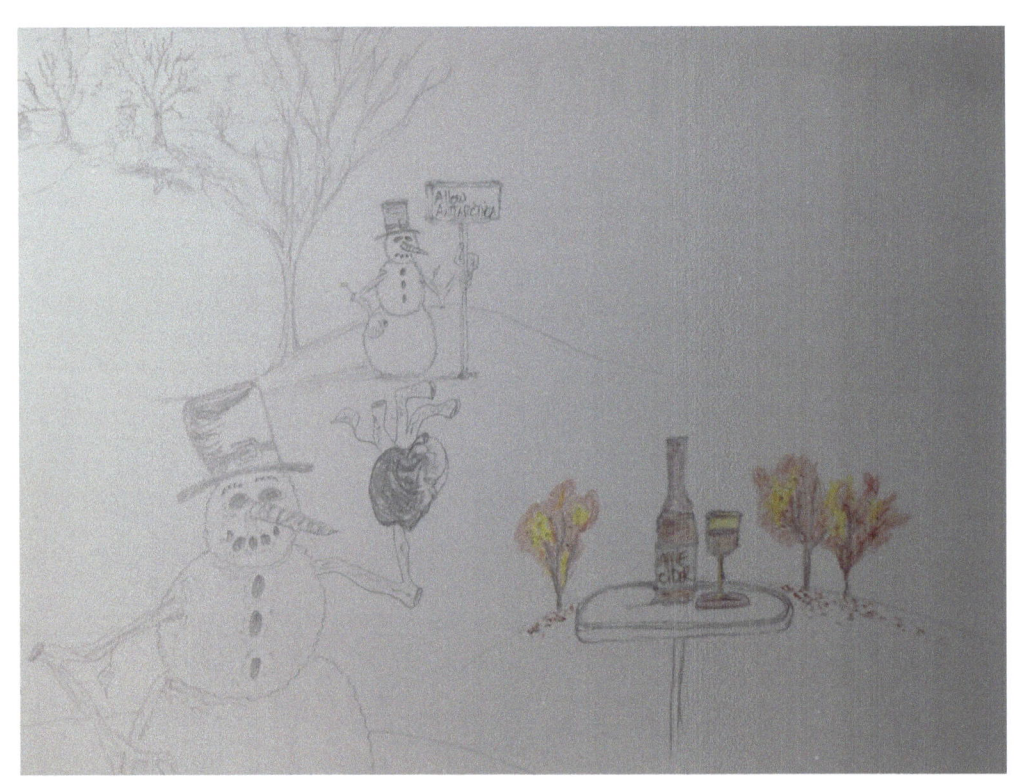

Snow in Ny, Autumn   2018   14 inches x 11 inches

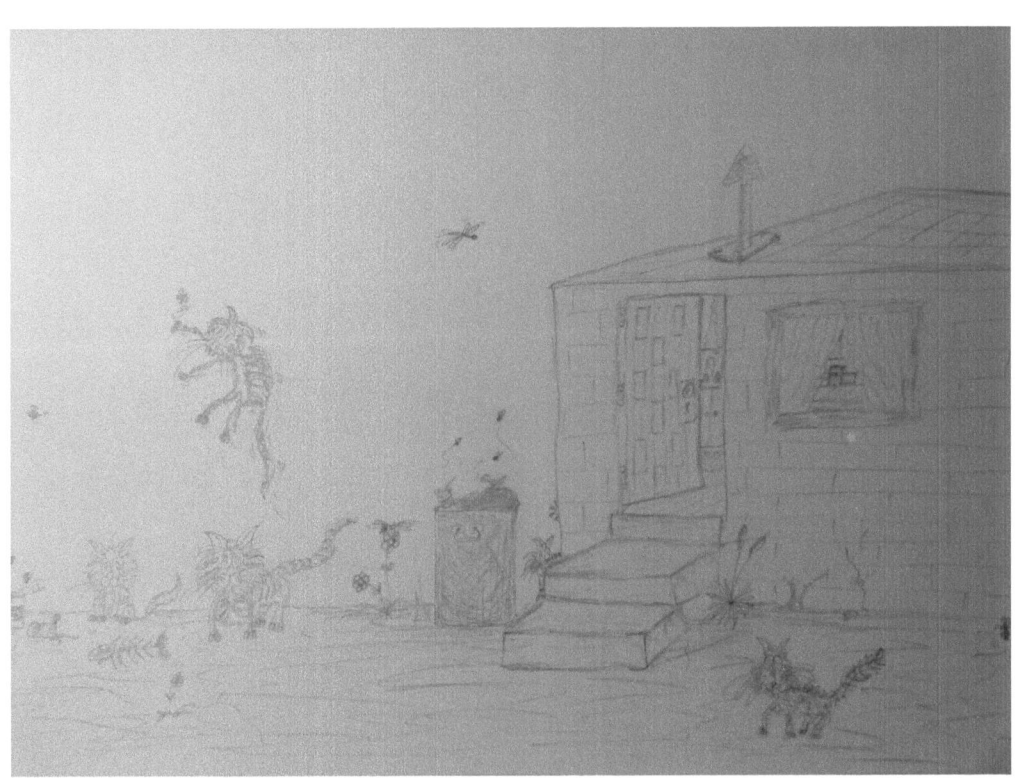

Unfinished Wayward Kitties   2019   14 inches x 11 inches

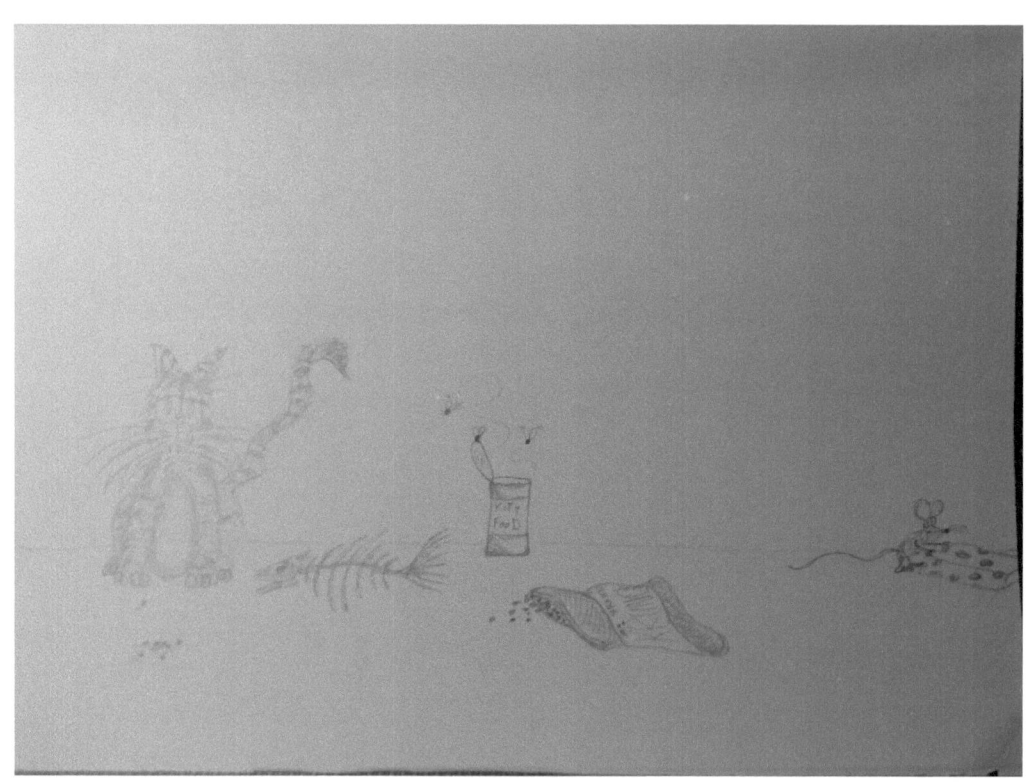

Unfinished Spoiled Fat Cat   2019   14 inches x 8 inches

Entertain yourself! It will bring a smile to everyone around you. Thanks for making it to the end of this book. Hope you enjoyed it as much as I enjoyed creating these images. As aways, have fun.
．．．．．．．．．．．．．．．．．．．．．．．．．．．．．．Breece A. Perry

Index

Introduction	Page 2
Tea Cups and Bottle on Plate	Page 3
Fishing the Coffee Canyon	Page 4
Moving on From Landscapes	Page 5
Lemonade in the Shallows	Page 6
Constant Elevation	Page 7
Sprouts	Page 8
Hey There Ladies	Page 9
Seen and Not Heard	Page 10
Southern Trees	Page 11
School Flat Out Boring	Page 12
Broken Landscape	Page 13
Pencil Ink Triangles	Page 14
Seasonal Swing	Page 15
Change, Dream Big	Page 16
Pinhead Sprout	Page 17
Some Kind of Evil	Page 18
Sea Scape	Page 19
Pull My Finger	Page 20
Glass Peace	Page 21
Space Plant Harvest Moon	Page 22
Jester Balance	Page 23
Unfinished Lovers	Page 24
Life Sucker	Page 25
Distortion Sphere	Page 26
Graduation Only Weeks Away	Page 27
Checkered Board	Page 28
Unfinished Hair Chop	Page 29
Breece Tries to Draw	Page 30
Blah…Blah…Blah…	Page 31
Lines Over Shapes	Page 32
Neck Bone the Trucker	Page 33
Billboard in Phoenix	Page 34
Cronomer (top) Drop Dead (bottom)	Page 35
Charcoal Corn Snake	Page 36
Bone Shaker and Martini	Page 37
Unfinished Brains on Sale	Page 38
Unfinished Lou	Page 39
Unfinished Bone Face	Page 40
Deferment Request	Page 41
Locked Out Dept. of Labor	Page 42
Tight Wired	Page 43
Unfinished Home Defense	Page 44
Unfinished The Day i Broke	Page 45
Snow in Ny, Autumn	Page 46
Unfinished Wayward Kitties	Page 47
Unfinished Spoiled Fat Cat	Page 48
Conclusion: Artist/ Author Sentiments	Page 49

www.ingramcontent.com/pod-product-compliance
Lightning Source LLC
Chambersburg PA
CBHW051219220526
45473CB00003B/1095